Re

"2020 has incited a flight or fight response for many entrepreneurs including myself. This can be helpful in times of acute stress, but Infinite Journey helps reground to the bigger picture and provides a framework of how to approach such dynamic times. The focus on a few clear but powerful principles and how they interact prompts powerful introspection. The concepts are easy to conceptualize but hard to implement; I'm excited to use the techniques outlined here and apply them to my own life challenges!" ~ **Harrison Hunter**, CTO MaestroQA, Forbes 30 Under 30 (2020)

"I have known Dr. Forsythe for over 50 years. She has always been the epitome of calm and positivity—the "real deal" as I like to say. She has a talent for looking people in the eye, listening carefully and acting with compassion and honesty. Her advice is always on the mark so I have no doubt that this book will be a useful and easy tool for anyone looking for extra help along their journey." ~ **Katherine Johnston Hutto**, former professional in the service of White House Chief of Staff to President Reagan, James A. Baker, III, for 5 years and to H.M. Queen Noor of Jordan for 10 years

"Dr. Moira Forsythe is a gifted communicator and has helped countless people, myself included, to realize their full potential. I know from experience that the concepts detailed in this book will help readers lead a more balanced and enriched life." ~ **Andre D. Spino-Smith,** CFO, South

Main Development, Managing Broker/ Co-Owner, South Main Realty

"Throughout my career I have found working with a good coach is so important for gaining clarity and seeing things from a broader perspective. I like that this book has exercises and tips for how to explore the concepts of Clarity, Courage, and Congruence. Trust the process and let this book ignite the fire and magic in your life." ~ **Ruthie Bolton**, 2x Olympic Gold medalist Team USA Women's Basketball, 2x WNBA All Star, 3x Hall of Famer

"Infinite Journey is a detailed inner-space road map. This important book arrives at a time when good, clear, useful 'maps' can be difficult to come by. Dr. Forsythe has the unique ability to open up new worlds of possibilities and potentials while being down to earth and inclusive of the diversity of her client-base. This is a rare book that will improve your mindset, your skill-set, and your life if you will simply follow the map provided within." ~ **Cheryl Page**, CCRP, Director of Clinical Research at Valley View Hospital, Glenwood Springs, CO

"Against the backdrop of a raging pandemic, Dr. Moira Forsythe and Mark Dockendorff offer valuable tools to help us individually and collectively find our rhythm and cadence during times of uncertainty; bringing our lives back to a state of congruence. Using resources gleaned from years of coaching clients, this book challenges the reader to be curious, to seek clarity, and to act courageously whilst navigating the journey of life." ~ **Tiffany S. Hayden**, Assistant Athletic Director for Diversity, Equity and Inclusion/WBB

Liaison, University of Kentucky Athletics

"I don't think there's anyone who wouldn't benefit from reading this book. Dr. Forsythe and Mark Dockendorff are coaches who really care about people and want to give them the tools to create better lives and opportunities. This book offers 4 Concepts to be explored as a guide for your journey during these uncertain times and the current times of unrest in our country and the world. Well worth reading and sharing with others." ~ **Gerald Roulette**, former NFL player, Kansas City Chiefs, contemporary abstract artist, art teacher, and high school coach

"Infinite Journey: Creating Calm in Times of Chaos offers a 4-step strategy of continuous exploration and growth to help us navigate unknown territory. Sharing examples from their personal and professional experiences, Dr. Forsythe and Mark Dockendorff help us overcome the challenges and chaos that we may encounter in our life journey." ~ **Akemi Chan-Imai,** MA, Certified Nonprofit Professional

INFINITE JOURNEY

Creating Calm in Times of Chaos

Dr. Moira M. Forsythe
Mark J. Dockendorff

Powerful You! PUBLISHING
Sharing Wisdom ~ Shining Light

Infinite Journey
Creating Calm in Times of Chaos

Published by: Powerful You! Inc. USA
powerfulyoupublishing.com

Library of Congress Control Number: 2020924209

Dr. Moira M. Forsythe and Mark J. Dockendorff – First Edition

ISBN: 978-1-7356579-1-2

First Edition December 2020

BODY MIND & SPIRIT / Inspiration & Personal Growth

Dedication

To all who wander, wonder, and are not lost,
may your Journeys be filled with
love, joy, and abundance.

Table of Contents

Acknowledgments & Gratitude

~ Dr. Moira M. Forsythe

I am deeply grateful to be able to live in, connect with, and be inspired by the amazing high country in which I reside. The wilderness of the world has called to me for over five decades. It continually fuels my passion for preservation and my curiosity for exploration; brings me strong breezes that clear confusion and leave new clarity; and challenges me with choices that require courage on a regular basis. The lessons learned on the dirt trails of the forest always have value for the other areas of my life.

I am grateful to the man who instilled the sense of adventure and joy for travel in me at a very young age—my father, John Winston Forsythe. Traveling thousands of miles from his island birthplace, he faced the obstacles in his numerous journeys with a sense of humor and a huge capacity for joy. His sharing of stories of the long line of adventurers from which I come has fueled and inspired my confidence to trust my own wanderlust as a true path to follow.

I am grateful to the many coaches, clients, teachers, and fellow travelers I have met along the way. Their insights, perspectives, and experiences have been a beacon of confirmation for the universal direction towards Love in which we are all traveling.

I also want to acknowledge my beautiful daughters, Alexandra and Danielle, for their support and encouragement even when my curiosity and choices took me far from them. Their unwavering acceptance of my ever-evolving interests gifted me the emotional space to weave those adventures together into a dynamic magic carpet on which to ride as I continue along this Journey.

I'd like to thank our publisher Sue Urda for her clear guidance and support throughout this process. It has been her expertise and confidence in this project that has allowed it to come into being with ease and grace.

And finally, I'd like to thank my creative companion and cohort, Mark Dockendorff, who has embraced the crazy with curiosity and courage and a willingness to come play with me as we crafted this book. The laughter we shared along the way added great joy to the work of getting it all out onto paper.

Moira M. Forsythe
Americus, Colorado

Acknowledgments & Gratitude

~ Mark J. Dockendorff

I would like to express my gratitude to Moira, for all her energy and dedication in co-creating the magic of this book. Here's to more expansion and playful collaboration as we share this cause with others.

I would also like to express my gratitude to Jeffery Kern, my best friend and journey companion. He has been an amazing partner to share and create with on every level, including with the graphics in this book.

With great reverence, I honor my amazing mother, who has always guided me gently and with a courageous heart. I am so blessed to have you as my loving Mamusia Krystyna, always and forever!

I would also like to give special thanks to all who shared their inspiring stories with me during the research leg of this projcct. I appreciate your openness and generosity of spirit.

Mark Dockendorff
Okemos, Michigan

THE INFINITE JOURNEY

There is a private chamber in the soul
That knows a great secret

Of which no tongue can speak.

Your existence my dear, O love my dear,
Has been sealed and marked

"Too sacred," "too sacred," by the Beloved –
To ever end!

Indeed God
Has written a thousand promises
All over your heart

That say,
Life, life, life
Is far too sacred to
Ever end.

Excerpt from the poem, God's Bucket, by Hafiz,
translation by Daniel Ladinsky

Introduction

AN IDEA IS BORN

As we write this, people the world over are seeking ways to deal with ever-increasing uncertainty, social upheaval, and even chaos. Indeed, there are ways of maintaining direction, focus, and joy even as distractions rise around us. These strategies draw from the fields of professional coaching, positive psychology, and spirituality with universal principles that transcend any specific circumstance.

The ideas herein challenge some of the traditional implementation of these strategies as we ask readers to consider that life is not a game, either infinite or finite, but rather a journey. Games inherently imply winning and losing, and no matter how cleverly we state our definition or perception of those terms, the collective subconscious is deeply rooted in the concepts of either/or, or "us versus them." The tension created by these terms energetically is unavoidable, palpable, and ultimately sabotaging, both individually and collectively.

The concept of a journey, on the other hand, brings us to the mindset of traveling together, not as competitors but as fellow adventurers—exploring, learning, and adapting as our respective environments demand. Travelers tend to embrace novelty and discovery with a curiosity that is expansive and exciting. Oftentimes a measure of courage is required to stay the course on a given journey or to venture further into the unknown than planned. Shifting circumstances (i.e. terrain, weather, companions, energy, or supplies) challenge the sourcing of deeper strengths and ingenuity and demand humility in the process of decision-making—all of which are valuable skillsets for navigating daily life.

As a former mountaineering guide, I learned to make sure that all members of a given party were always accounted for, encouraged at whatever pace they undertook, and tended to with appropriate levels of care specific to their individual needs. Moving together along a trail often brings individuals of vastly different backgrounds together with a common goal, each with their own unique reasons for the experience. Often the pace of the whole is set by the slowest participant. When that was not the case, I, as the leader, made sure to be at both the front of the group and at the rear in equal measure. At the end of each day everyone would gather to share their individual experiences along the same path. The development of unity of purpose within unique engagement of the process was a valuable learning that would carry over into many areas of our lives.

The spiritual traditions of the world, no matter how loosely or tightly structured they may be, all have some perspective of "what comes next." It is this concept of a continuation of some element of our being that has fueled the idea around an Infinite Journey.

We propose that journeying though life is much the same as journeying along that path—we move along with our fellow travelers, each of us striving to reach various waystations we identify for ourselves. This journey continues each day into the next toward an ultimate transition that carries us forward into even more unknown territory. When we take these steps from an expanded personal consciousness, we can create a journey that, although challenging at times, becomes an experience of learning, growth, connectedness, and joy.

Danish philosopher Kierkegaard postulated that each individual, not society or religion, is responsible for giving meaning to life and living it passionately and authentically. In this collection of stories and tools, we attempt to bring together a variety of techniques from several different disciplines of thought, many backed by academic studies, that support us in the process of living. Indeed, our clients who have used these techniques have gained better clarity, deeper calm, and increased personal satisfaction in all areas of life. Our goal is to inspire readers to explore and experience some of these strategies and begin to track the impact on their lives.

The concepts contained herein are intended to stimulate expanded thinking on the part of the reader. At the end of each section are exercises that will help to sharpen awareness of one's values and the ways by which one can make conscious choices to live more fully into those values. This is part of the foundation on which life acquires meaning.

These are the tools in your personal travel bag.

We are all in this together, and together we CAN create a world in which all humans are living into their potential, contributing to, as well as enjoying, a more peaceful, productive, and prosperous world.

In the words of Oliver Wendell Holmes, "The great thing in this world is not so much where we are, but in what direction we are moving."

Let's do this!

THE INFINITE JOURNEY

Those of you who are experienced hikers or outdoorspeople are familiar with the concept of The 10 Essentials—or the items all adventurers are mandated to have on their person when venturing into the wild. They are also highly recommended for shorter day hikes as they bring an element of preparedness for any eventuality to the outing, which in turn brings an increased confidence to explore and enjoy.

Similar in function are the circles of attributes ("Bubbles") you will find around each of the four components we explore in this book. They are tools that bring value to the experience of being on this amazing journey we call "Life." We have chosen attributes or qualities that we feel are significantly connected to the fundamental skills within each component. Some build skill, some get developed as a skill, some are simply outcomes you might experience by engaging with the central concept. In keeping with the notion that we are all at different places along the path, there will be different tools and skills that are most useful at each stage of progression.

We know these tools work based our experience working with hundreds of individuals seeking to find strengths for themselves, their projects, and their dreams. That said, you should use our suggestions as just that: suggestions. Know that there are many others, and we encourage readers to take the time to explore what resonates for themselves. You might find that doing so expands your awareness around what is most useful for you on your journey. Enjoy!

CORE ENERGY COACHING: AN OVERVIEW

There are many definitions of coaching being presented in the world today, and in the US alone there are over two hundred coaching programs one might enroll in. One important commonality among them is that coaching is grounded in the principle that individuals are resourceful, creative, and capable of crafting powerful solutions to challenges they may face in life. Coaching provides a nonjudgmental container for empowering action-oriented strategies that serve to transform potential into reality more quickly and effectively, in both times of challenge and times of ease. It is inspirational, compassionate, disruptive, and expansive. Coaching is a process which not only assists individuals in setting clear goals but in the achievement of those goals as well.

> *"Masterful coaching involves helping people in groups transform themselves, their communities, and their world."*
>
> ~ Robert Hargrove, Masterful Coaching

While as certified coaches Mark and I incorporate a range of trainings in varied disciplines of human development, it is the common certification as Core Energy coaches (ELI-MP) that initially drew us together as collaborators. The central concept from which the strategies of Energy Leadership Index specialists spring is that we are all energetic systems functioning in physical form, in a physically structured world. The basis for cohesive functioning is dependent upon recognizing this aspect of reality and choosing supportive components to maintain the energy systems within a healthy, expansive, "building" state.

It is important—vital, in fact—that this energetic system is impacted by our level of consciousness as reflected by thoughts, emotions, beliefs, values, and the behaviors that spring from these invisible processes.

"All thoughts have an energetic consequence."
~ iPEC Foundations Manual

The fields of professional coaching and positive psychology have identified core thoughts associated with outcomes that are desirable, affirming, and forward-moving, and those which are not. These are the "consequences," referenced in the quote above, and they show up as the perception of and interactions we have with various circumstances in our lives. This partially explains how two individuals can have vastly different recall around the same event (i.e. as either disastrous, productive, or simply "interesting").

Core Energy coaches are trained to support an individual's recognition of where their energetic state is overall and where it may go in response to various stimulus in their life. This recognition can also be termed "self-awareness." There are many tools that purport to enhance this awareness, and again we encourage readers to source out resources that resonate for them and will potentially bring greater levels of inner health and peacefulness.

We then empower clients to craft uniquely appropriate response strategies that serve to support higher states of energy functioning. Through this process they begin to create a foundational state of being that is more creative, adaptable, and joy-filled. For those engaged in business ventures this foundation leads to higher levels of productivity and satisfaction as well.

Throughout this book we have attempted to simplify some of the techniques and perspectives we have found to be most useful in engaging with this process of our own "energy management." Much like how we choose tools to carry with us on an outdoor adventure, we can choose from these tools to manage whatever challenges may present themselves in this phase of the Infinite Journey.

We have also presented a progression through several skill-building stages that is self-generating and repeating. Movement through the stages is interconnected and spirals around back onto itself with expanded vision and engagement. You may find comfort at any point along the way and choose to stay there awhile; you may also take alternate paths in parallel to the ones presented here. Whatever you choose, you will surely find new insights, unique to you and valuable to others as they too seek their way back to joy.

INFINITE JOURNEY

We have expanded upon the 3D Coaching process developed by Dr. Forsythe to include four principles, shown in the Bubble above, which enhance personal awareness and social advancements. Moving through these areas of Curiosity, Clarity, Courage, and Congruence is what can bring us to the discovery of new pathways through this journey called life.

In addition to making these concepts accessible, we would like for your exploration of this material to be fun and a bit playful. We encourage you to feel free to enhance your visual engagement with the material by coloring the various circle diagrams and using the lined pages at the end of each chapter to record your reflections or add other resources you may find as you explore a concept. Date your entries and notes so you can refer back to the concepts over time and see what progress has occurred.

Our ultimate goal is to empower people to create lives filled with joy, peace, abundance, and power that is congruent with their values and constructively connected to the larger world. We call this **Inspired Living**, and we wish that for all who enter here.

"Instructions for living a life.
Pay attention. Be astonished. Tell about it."
~ Mary Oliver

Chapter One

The Spark That Ignited This Journey

I would like to share a story from early 2020 that illustrates the benefit that embodying the concepts explored in this book can have.

In February, my most precious and only granddaughter was stricken with a medical challenge that threw us into a labyrinth of confusion, misdiagnoses, and deep winter travel over numerous icy mountain passes in search of resolution. It also became, despite the fears and uncertainty, a family journey of love, compassion, and pooling of strengths as we rallied around the smallest in our tribe.

We gathered together as we waited to hear the results of seemingly endless tests and supported one another as this young child went through multiple surgeries, prolonged infections, and sleepless hospital nights. As I watched alongside my daughter and her husband as their tender four-year-old was poked, pricked, monitored, and medicated, I became *curious* as to how other less connected families on the ward were managing. How were they finding the balance and *courage* to maintain calm and strength amidst their own scary pediatric dramas?

Having been raised in an environment of inquiry and discovery, my daughter was able to be the courageous advocate needed to navigate the processes of this medical mystery. Her knowing that *clarity* was possible empowered her to continue pushing through the daunting challenges of this journey until *congruence* was found, literally saving my granddaughter's life.

Our hospital stays rolled right into the beginnings of the Covid-19 eruption in the United States. Since we were already on high "infection prevention alert," our transition to new coronavirus restrictions was fairly seamless. As our nine-person, three-generation family collective had also been traveling together, and been exclusive of others, for weeks, we were able to continue much as we had before—with regular recovery hikes on the beautiful mountain trails we call home, sleepovers at "Gma's" cabin in the woods, and convivial family meals. The two school-aged members of our family were not affected by ensuing school closures, as they had already been living the new routines we had constructed around this medical journey.

I was keenly aware that many people were experiencing much more abrupt and drastic changes to their daily lives. As the pandemic unfolded day by day, sometimes minute by minute, the number of folks trying to find clarity amidst the confusion increased exponentially. I was *curious* as to how the newly-imposed rules of social isolation were affecting those without the kind of access to restorative activities we enjoyed.

It became *clear* to me that some of the techniques that I use to stay grounded and regularly share with my coaching clients would be of value to others. Now I was asking myself how I could best share my own abundance of spirit with others who might benefit from it. The question prompted many hours of deep reflection.

I shared this mission with other coaches who were seeking ways of using their unique talents to be of service during this time, and found their eagerness to join forces exciting and gratifying. This was the inspiration and the catalyst for Coaches That Care, an initiative to bring the power of coaching, at no cost, to those who needed it.

The coaches who participated were extremely generous, donating thousands of dollars of professional coaching services, including individual support calls. Yet, as the impacts of the global pandemic dragged on for weeks, then months, it became *clear* that even more assistance was needed and would be for quite some time. It was also clear that in order to keep delivering useful resources I would have to find personal *courage* to step out of my comfort zone. I am a relatively reclusive and private person by nature, more comfortable on quiet trails in the backcountry than brightly lit stages in conference halls, or in this case, hosting Zoom meetings with large numbers of attendees.

> *"Change and growth take place when a person has risked himself and dares to become involved with experimenting with his own life."*
>
> ~ Herbert A. Otto, author and psychologist

This book is the result of my experimenting—my effort to bring some of the resources and guidance tools used within more formal coaching practices to whomever might desire to try them. It is designed to empower ownership of the design of one's experience and responses in both times of calm and chaos.

In reviewing the essence of the above experiences—my family's health journey and the creation of Coaches That Care—the presence of four key elements began to stand out. These same elements are foundational to the strategies I generally use, in progression, with clients. We typically begin with CURIOSITY around what is true, what is desired, what is needed to get to what is desired, and how it might be implemented. We then explore developing the CLARITY achieved from this inquiry process and allow creativity and positive perspective to shape what emerges as potential strategies for moving forward. The client must then find the COURAGE to "step into action" and implement actual changes. Though the amount of courage required varies from case to case, it is always present whenever something new is being crafted. The result is the CONGRUENCE, or coherence with self, that emerges as we step authentically into our deepest truths. Whether the challenge is large or small, on the other side of the process is peace, joy, and an appreciation for the learnings the journey can bring.

WHY "INFINITE" AND WHY "JOURNEY"

Mark was engaged in a conversation with his mother, Krys, that highlighted our use of the term "Infinite" as relevant for so many, whether they are currently exploring these concepts or not. Krys, a devout and lifelong Catholic practitioner, was on her way to church to deposit funds for a mass to be said in remembrance of a departed relative. Mark was curious as to the value of such a "prayer-for-purchase" transaction and asked his mother what her desired outcome might be. Krys responded that it was to insure, or at least increase the chances of, the eventual smooth transition into an afterlife experience more desirous than whatever other options might be on the spiritual docket. She also expressed the belief that the person on the other plane of existence might "feel" this consideration from her directly and somehow be able to appreciate the remembrance.

With curiosity and great respect, Mark began to engage Krys in a dialogue about how adopting a perspective of continuity of experience might serve one while in this present life. He spoke of how this might support the travel of one's essence, or soul, into other dimensions once physicality was done. Such a perspective might thus encourage one to focus on the development of attributes such as kindness, generosity, gratitude, and service while "here," so as to invite gracious experiences into their lives and gift those "left behind" with energetic remembrances that were also uplifting and positive. The discussion also covered some aspects of quantum energetics, which for Krys resulted in an opening of consciousness as to the different possibilities for how we are all connected, eternally and infinitely. Mark came away with an appreciation for his mother's desire to remain connected to this person who had transitioned and with deeper clarity around how to introduce some expanded ways of thinking to others.

Throughout history humans have, in various ways, contemplated and embraced the idea that there is more "out there" than the mundane material world we perceive around us. Countless hours of meditation and psychological and spiritual attention have been spent trying to figure out "what's next," and the concept of infinite consciousness has been interwoven into legends, myths, and cultural belief systems worldwide. How we choose to interact with that concept inevitably shapes the world dynamics we create. Many spiritual traditions acknowledge and honor aspects of generational energies that carry forward for eons. Cultures spend many of their social assets on creating legacy monuments and artifacts to be passed on in perpetuity. As individuals, we often spend much time and financial resources planning our own legacy to ensure we'll be remembered for generations beyond our tenure here.

Many deep thinkers of the day contend that a number of our social structures no longer serve humanity's collective wellbeing. Moreover, many of the global systems of living things are reflecting the generally dysfunctional policies we subscribe to as the dominant species on the planet. This prompts many to ponder "what else could be possible." Are there different ways in which we could be interacting with one another and advancing social structures so as to build more harmony, equity, and joy for all? The general malaise of discontent has led to more widespread protest and civil unrest than has been seen in over half a century, as well as a rampant uncertainty and anxiety about where we are headed.

However, when we view our current state of affairs as merely one section of a bigger "Journey," we can begin to shape new strategies for moving through it most constructively. As stated earlier, the energy that we tend to bring to a Journey is very different from the energy we bring to a game. Our perceptions—for example, that of an adventure versus a win-or-lose game—affects how we choose to engage with the processes of the experience, and thus the integrity of the outcome. When we embrace a notion of traveling with others, we move from a comparative perspective to a collaborative one. The quality of synergism begins to expand, and fresh creative strategies emerge that are inclusive and less judgmental.

Letting go of the construct of a game, with all its rules, boundaries, limitations, successes, and failures, allows for the emergence of new dynamics to play with. We begin to explore the realm of "what else is possible" with no constraints impeding the process of discovery. Curiosity becomes infused with courage as the point of the journey becomes to "see what comes next." Energy can be put into clarification of values so that choices can be made from a place that serves to strengthen the soul and enable joy in greeting the challenges that appear along the way.

While this requires focus and effort, it can also bring relief as coping skills increase and ease of experience emerges. We hope you enjoy going on this journey with us and that you will find something of value here that enhances your travels.

> *"...everywhere in the world are ordinary people willing to confront despair, power, and incalculable odds in order to restore some semblance of grace, justice, and beauty to this world."*
>
> ~ Paul Hawken

"The future belongs to the curious. The ones who are not afraid to try it, explore it, poke at it, question it and turn it inside out."

~ Long Island Explorium,
Children's Museum of Science & Engineering

Chapter Two

Curiosity

Seven months after the medical crisis I shared in the last chapter, my darling granddaughter and I found ourselves on a trail hike in the mountains above Frisco, Colorado. It was a glorious, late-summer day, and a hike was the perfect way to occupy ourselves while her mother took her older brother for a check-up at the dentist's. We made our way up a steep access trail that teed into a well-worn pathway which then split into two different sections of the woods. There I shared with her the story of our hike to this same point when she was just a toddler. That day, because she had been so little, this was as far as we had gotten before heading back to the cars below. Now, I asked her, "Which way should we go? Left or right?"

She stopped for a minute, taking in the feeling of power of being able to decide the next hour of our time together. Then, after visually evaluating the long meadow to the left and the uphill, hidden trail into tall aspen groves on the right, she burst out "Right!"

I responded, "Excellent. I have always been curious about where this trail goes."

I wish I had brought a camera to capture the look of pure delight on her face as she turned to me and enthusiastically said, "I *love* being curious!" before skipping up the trail with glee.

The exchange made me laugh out loud as I reflected on how as adults we become so removed from expressing the feelings of pure joy at such simple choices. During the course of our hour-plus trek into unknown territory, dark due to the density of aspens, challenging due to the angle of incline, and exciting due to the ever-present possibility of encountering migrating wildlife, we laughed, looked for woodland fairies, inspected rosehips, and gathered golden aspen leaves of all sizes to tape into our nature journals once we got back home.

It is always a treat to witness someone being excited about exploring the outdoors, being curious about what is "just around the bend"—for me, it is symbolic of the wholehearted engagement in living so common in the young. To share that experience as an adventure with someone I love and who loves me as unconditionally was an energetic bonus I shall always treasure.

We crossed paths with only two other groups of paired travelers on the trail that day—"grownups" in full covid mask regalia, looking alarmed at the prospect of having to pass others on the trail. (Truly, the path was wide enough to safely social-distance by simply stepping into the trees a bit). There was an air of seriousness and solemnity that both my granddaughter and I remarked upon after we moved past them. Our giggling and spontaneous, unstructured song bursts seemed to surprise both sets of hikers.

Were they not seeing the incredible beauty of the quaking aspen all around us? Was not the brilliant high altitude sunshine infusing them with verve and delight? Were the masks impeding their ability to fully inhale and enjoy the crisp clean fall mountain air? We unapologetically shared gleeful greetings and joy-filled calls to "have a great day" and "enjoy your hike" as we stepped off to allow the pairs to pass. I hope our delight was contagious to some degree as the energy of the moment is all we ever really have access to at any place in time. At that place, in that time, it was extraordinary.

RECONNECTING WITH CURIOSITY

As professional coaches we are trained to first and foremost remain in a state of curiosity about our clients and their concerns, their challenges, their lives, and their work. We use techniques of open-ended inquiry to support them in developing clarity for themselves around specific issues, which then allows for the creation of unique strategies that will serve them most authentically. What I have discovered from serving hundreds of clients over the years is that many adults are surprised at the very process of inquiry. Many have suspended that activity of questioning "the way things are" in order to see what else might be possible. Many have never experienced deep curiosity from another around what their unique heartfelt perspectives on an issue might be.

All great explorers start with a sense of curiosity. This level of focused awareness leads them to the new horizons that both expand their outer lives and tap into the deeper levels of their inner resources.

Curiosity sparks the imagination, develops awareness, and leads to discoveries that can expand the sense of what's possible. Having a sense that something other than current reality may exist as a potential experience fuels optimism and hope. Trusting that we can learn the process for connecting with, or even personally creating, a dynamic view of the world can instill a sense of personal empowerment that is a key component of the resilience we all need as chaos emerges around us.

The courage to be curious leads to clarity around purpose, goals, and values, which in turn empowers choices that create congruence in experience. This leads to a deeper trust in the process, which continues to spiral around in an ever expanding trajectory towards Enlightenment/Joy/ Fulfillment/ Peace. Discovering which answer is uniquely ours is part of the fun in the journey.

That said, curiosity is just one essential component to living an empowered, joyful life. Let's go back to the explorer analogy. Not too long ago, whenever one set out to reach a new destination, they would pack a map or road atlas, a compass if it was a wilderness journey and, of course, a bag of snacks for sustenance along the way. In other words, they were curious, but also used tools to guide them on their path. Today, the host of digital wayfinding tools like GPS and google maps have made traveling much lighter, yet most experienced travelers know they may need to still call on their skills of awareness and observation in order to stay on course. The same is true with the journey of life, where we need to use self-reliance to navigate through the incredible amount of information—much of it inaccurate—and distracting stimuli that conspire to throw us off track.

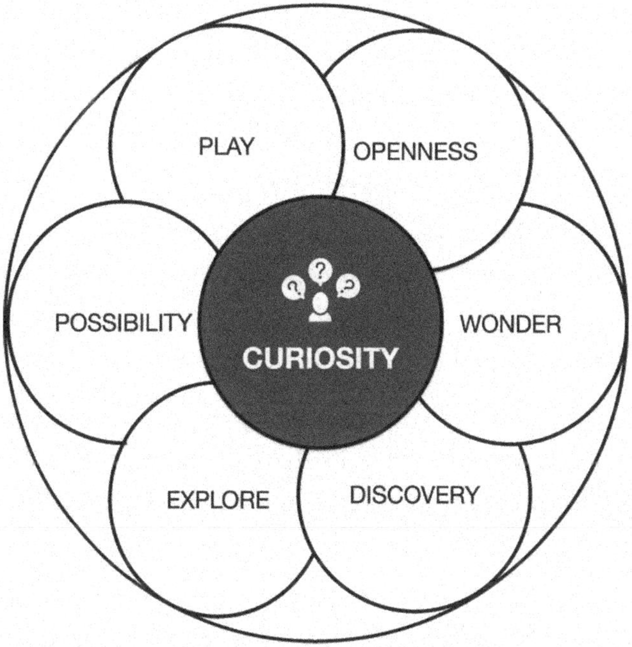

CURIOSITY BUBBLE

We encourage readers to take each of the words in the Curiosity Bubble and create a definition that is relevant for them. In deepening your understanding of the components of curiosity you can begin to recognize where you might add more tools for yourself.

Here are some prompting questions to get you started:

1. **PLAY** – How often do you do something which has no obvious purpose but is simply fun? Consider where you might be able to add more occasions like that.

2. **OPENNESS** – How do you respond when someone inserts an unexpected activity into your day? Are you "open" to spontaneous changes or do you view them as an intrusion? How might you breathe into spontaneity with an attitude of curiosity instead of one of dread and resistance?

3. **WONDER** – What have you seen that caused you to "wonder" where it came from, how it was used, what the meaning of its purpose might be? How did you follow up on the unknown about something?

4. **DISCOVERY** – How deeply do you follow up on the unknown elements that cross your path? What subject, topic, or person would you like to know more about?

5. **EXPLORE** – When was the last time you walked or drove into an unfamiliar area just to see what was there? If safety is a concern for you, when was the last time you simply browsed without specificity in a local bookstore or museum? During the pandemic, museums are offering virtual touring of their collections, so find a location in another city or country that has these tours scheduled.

6. **POSSIBILITY** – Challenge yourself to look at projects you are currently engaged in, even if it as

mundane as folding clothes or washing dishes, and ask yourself, "What is another way I might do this? What else is possible here?" Begin to bring those questions to other choices that appear for you in the course of a week.

When working with business or fitness issues, use the question "How might__________ approach this challenge?" Fill in the blank with your most admired icon and see what genius thinking begins to flow!

SUPPORTING CURIOSITY

A Coaching Story

Katherine was a high-performing, driven young executive who was experiencing great anxiety and frustration at the pace of progress on several projects. She had envisioned 2020 as a year of accomplishment in both her business and personal life, and had set specific goals for expanding her family, building a new home with her husband, spearheading a newly formed non-profit as its executive director, and implementing several initiatives at work that would highlight her organizational skills while expanding resources for team members. Most of these plans, however, had been slowed or halted by the unexpected shutdowns in response to the global pandemic—at least, that was her primary complaint. Secondary was the subsequent lack of motivation Katherine reported creeping into most of her other daily routines. She was not exercising as she liked, she wasn't interested in her book clubs as much as usual, and her disappointment in changes to vacation plans created a rather grumpy attitude at home.

Although she was able to identify this malaise and the circumstances that had triggered it, she felt stymied as to how to change it. The more she felt the anxiety and frustration, the less able she was to shift those emotions, which only led to more anxiety and deeper levels of dissatisfaction. This self-fueling cycle of stagnation was beginning to impact Katherine's sleep patterns, her marriage, and her sense of self.

We discussed how it might be to evaluate the ideal scenarios she had crafted at the beginning of the year in light of what was now actually possible given the imposed restrictions. I tasked Katherine with asking "what else might be possible" for each area of her life in which she was feeling challenged. Then, using the skill of curiosity, with suspended judgment around the value of any particular insight that came up, she was to come up with two alternate "possibilities" for each area and create at least two "first steps" toward action in one of the possibilities.

Just the suggestion of beginning to imagine "what else" began to snap Katherine out of the doldrums that had gripped her spirit over the past few months. Daily activities began to feel brighter and her feelings of anticipation for productive outcomes began to become more optimistic. Each area of life that had seemed to plateau now took on new dynamism as Katherine focused on the aspects of what was truly present to work with and began to envision fresh ways of creating momentum in each.

This process of examination with curiosity, attainment of clarity, and then creation of action serves to provide both groundedness and calm, as well as energy and dynamism. When we embrace the concept that "how we do anything is how we do everything," the impacts of this type of inner shift in perspective carries into many areas of one's life organically. And just like the self-fueling cycle of stagnation, this cycle of curiosity and creativity begins to be self-supporting as well.

Having this process supported within the context of coaching sessions made it feel safer and easier for Katherine than if she had simply tried it on her own. We can each be that accountability and source of support for one another during challenging times by keeping our own levels of curiosity active. Like all skills, with repetition it becomes easier to do and progressively more fun to engage with. As we practice more and more, it can become an energetically embodied way of viewing the world and its interesting plot twists. Humor returns, joy expands, and self-confidence increases. Curiosity becomes our default mode and creative solutions become our normal output. We find we have greater courage to explore new options and, ultimately, gain inner congruence that increases our resilience for challenges across the board.

CURIOSITY:
desire to know, interest leading to inquiry

THE ART OF INQUIRY

Curiosity—about others, about the world around us, and about ourselves—is a characteristic we are born with. Just as it often gets trained out of us in school as we are told what to learn, it can also be re-instilled with a variety of techniques.

For example, scientists, counselors, and coaches all use processes of inquiry, both to further their own knowledge within their fields and to support the continued expansion of our knowing and wonder of life and the world around us. They are conscious of, and embrace, the imperfections present in most inquiry processes because they understand that it's not about perfection, but about the effort to discover. It's in the effort that revelation, advancement, and transformation occur.

Here are some strategies anyone can use to strengthen their curiosity skills.

1. Start off simple, with the most basic of curiosity questions about the world around you. Children are great models for this, as they pepper us with the repetitive "why?" about the way things are.
2. Begin your actual questions with open-ended starters: What...Who...How...If...?
   Examples:
   - What motivates me?
   - How does this make me feel?
   - What would it take to ________?
   - How does this choice serve to improve my life and/or the lives of others?
   - If money were no object, what would I do tomorrow?
   - What would I like to do more of?

The value of sharpening this skill cannot be emphasized enough. As we continue to encounter the many aspects of the unknown that are appearing in our world today, it becomes apparent that those with high levels of curiosity will be the ones to move most successfully through these challenges. Asking simple questions such as those above spark creativity and innovation, both of which have always been intimately connected to curiosity and the bravery required to engage it.

When Satya Nadella became CEO of Microsoft in 2014, he wrote an open letter to employees in which he stated, "I sign up for more online courses than I can complete. I fundamentally believe that if you are not learning new things, you stop doing great and useful things."

Mark and I embarked on a lengthy process of inquiry when discussing the creation of this book. We were curious about what value might be found in recording our experiences as coaches, as well as those we had observed from clients in response to some of the events of this year. We were curious about which of the many tools we use would be most helpful for those not familiar with the coaching process. We pondered how best to translate the sometimes esoteric perspectives of energy and quantum reality we played with in our conversations into easy-to-understand, useable concepts for others.

Just as important, we were keenly curious about how to make such a project fun.

EXERCISES TO INSPIRE CURIOSITY

> *"Research shows that curiosity increases with knowledge: the more we know, the more we want to know. To get this process started, "prime the pump" with some intriguing but incomplete information."*
>
> ~ from a 2013 article in the Brilliant Report

The following exercises are simple yet powerful ways to reconnect with your innate curiosity. It is not important which you choose, so long as you are inspired into action. Take the time to record your experiences (i.e. in journal or voice recording) so that you can recognize and reflect upon any changes over time.

OBSERVATION AS A PATH TO CURIOSITY

I tend to rearrange my rooms seasonally in order to capture the best natural lighting from month to month. This sometimes means moving reading chairs, tables, and plant stands to complete opposite ends of a space. Occasionally it means changing out area rugs and pieces of furniture for something that has been in the attic for a while, as well as all the accessories—tabletop adornments, plants, pictures, and books—that go with those room anchors. I then move on to the outdoor spaces, moving lawn chairs, windchimes, statuaries, potted plants, and favorite items in view of windows in the same way.

One of my favorite aspects of this solar alignment activity is asking my grandchildren what differences they notice about the spaces when they come to visit. Their environmental curiosity is easy to ignite after the first snowfall, when we search for signs of animal movement in fresh white blankets of snow. The subsequent research into winter habits, migration patterns, hibernation habits, shelter-building, footprint identification and more provides hours of discovery that births even more curiosity.

BEGIN YOUR JOURNEY TO GREATER CURIOSITY BY EXPLORING THE SURROUNDINGS MOST EASILY AVAILABLE TO YOU.

Engage in an observation process by creating a consistent routine. It can be as simple as sitting on a rock or a step right outside your door, or a walk through your yard, neighborhood, or local park. Make an effort to notice what is and what changes.

Have a small notebook handy (or use the "Notes" or Voice Memo apps on your smartphone) to record insights that arise in the moment, and to which you can later refer back to further your discoveries. Take a picture of the same tree or rock or vista each week so you can compare subtle changes that happen over time. Share this discovery process with someone else and encourage one another in engagement with new aspects of your chosen terrain. Through practice you will see a natural increase in your ability to notice and be curious. You will also begin to experience the joy of discovery, along with a growing fearlessness about the unknown.

This type of immersion has never been more important, given the world's ever-increasing engagement with a technology-driven style of work and play. We are natural creatures and must make time to support those elements of ourselves if we wish to maintain wellness.

As Rachel Carson so eloquently put it, "There is something infinitely healing in the repeated refrains of nature." As an inveterate outdoorswoman I know that although these refrains may repeat, they are never identical in their melody. As climate changes accelerate on our planet it is even more significant to notice these refrains, their changes, and be curious about them.

For more ideas on how to deepen this practice of observation and interface with the world around us, take a look at *Reclaiming the Wild Soul: How Earth's Landscapes Restore Us to Wholeness* by Mary Reynolds Thompson. It is filled with prompts and suggestions for accessing the inspirations available from the full range of environments we may find ourselves in.

GET TO KNOW A FAMILIAR STRANGER:

Choose someone with whom you interact on a regular basis but do not know personally (i.e. your mailperson, delivery person, grocery clerk, or local librarian) and begin to connect with questions that will expand your knowing of that person.

Respectful curiosity is almost always welcomed by those being questioned. Limit your inquiries to one or two general interest questions at a time: How is your day going? What is the best thing to happen so far today? What are you looking forward to over the weekend? How's your health/energy today? Do you have any children? Do you have any pets? How long have you been doing this work?

You can often preface the more personal questions with the phrase: "I was just curious about…"

Continue this gentle inquiry process for at least two weeks, noticing the emotions that arise within you. Also notice the reactions, and any changes to them, in the other person to your curiosity.

After two weeks, ask your "interviewee" how it has felt for them to be in the conversation with you.

RESOURCES ON CURIOSITY:

There are several books to consider that validate the importance of nurturing curiosity and/or share examples of how others have lived into their own curiosity about things around them. ANY books by or about explorers are a great place to start. Think about which of our natural environs sparks interest for you—oceans, mountains, forests, formal gardens, windswept deserts, or jungles—and search online for books about explorers of those regions. You are bound to find some interesting material!

Here are few of my personal favorites:

- *Soul of An Octopus: A Surprising Exploration into the Wonder of Consciousness,* by Sy Montgomery (2014)
- *My First Summer in the Sierra,* by John Muir (1911)
- *Everest, The West Ridge*, Thomas E. Hornbein (1965, 1980)
- *The Spell of the Rockies*, Enos Mills (1911)

Reading stories of adventuring to youngsters will also reinforce your own connection to the process of curiosity, as well as theirs. For a list of wonderful list of recommendations and activities for infants through early readers, visit www.growingbookbybook.com.

"More important than the quest for certainty is the quest for clarity."

~ Francois Gautier

Chapter Three

Clarity

CLARITY: *the quality of being coherent and intelligible; the quality of being clear and easy to understand, see, or hear*

FINDING CLARITY

Numerous thought leaders and modern psychologists hold to the theory that one of the primary drivers for humans is the need for certainty. As knowledge and certainty are inextricably linked, it is easy to assume that the vast amounts of information accessible to us today helps to fill that need; however, the opposite may actually be the case. Given the speed at which tools and concepts are evolving, what is "known" to be stable and valid today may not be held entirely true tomorrow, making certainty a tenuous concept on which to rely.

Moreover, for the past three hundred-plus years, man's migratory behavior around the world (along with a great deal of progress) has occurred not due to certainty, but because of *courage amidst uncertainty*. While some cultural relocation was necessitated by conflict or geographic disaster, it was always influenced or guided by those steeped in adventure and curiosity, with a desire to experience something new. Surely the genetic imprint of those wandering explorers remains somewhere within each of us today.

While we may not always experience certainty, we can achieve clarity about what we want and how we might get there. We propose that one way to do this is by adopting the explorer's mindset. If we could embrace the idea of an ever-changing landscape, with twists, turns and the possibility of hidden features around every bend, we might better equip our psyches for the true nature of the journey we are on. If we were able to view this one life as a constantly unfolding adventure, bringing newness and challenge at unpredictable moments, it might encourage us to work on developing skills that empower us to meet those challenges with confidence and anticipation instead of with dread and resistance. We could then choose how we interface with various surprises and uncertainties, either with full engagement and creative thinking or simply as an observer, assessing the changes and calculating our best responses over time.

When you are clear about what is truly important for you and what qualities contribute to your sense of being "on purpose," it becomes easier to step into meaningful actions that move you forward in life. Higher degrees of self-awareness, and extended awareness of events around us, can sharpen our capacity for appropriate responsiveness that is healthy, dynamic, and productive. This applies equally to circumstances in life, business, family, nation, and the world. The courage required to make choices that may be deemed unpopular or even unwise in the eyes of others will come with a measure of inner assurance that you are staying in integrity with the values you have identified as important. Staying in integrity helps to keep us on paths that lead to great destinations.

The job of creating clarity around these values, and ultimately around choices that align with them, is solely an inside job. We are the ones responsible for how we support ourselves on this part of the journey. What we choose will either reinforce our resolve when the going gets tough or cause us to falter without a safety net to fall back on.

Having clarity gives us a foundation from which to handle the uncertainties of life events we all get impacted by from time to time. It helps us to realize that we are not our circumstances; we are how we respond within those circumstances. Self-awareness can give us the objective perspective to be creative, proactive, and forward moving amidst the sometimes chaotic overtones of uncertainty. Being able to transform uncertainty into adventure empowers us to experience more joy and fulfillment as we navigate that type of terrain.

Researcher and professor Brené Brown tells us that one of the pillars of courage we must call upon to keep moving is the skill of resilience—or knowing how to get up when we fall. And, if we are being bold, stepping courageously into action with our choices, we *will* fall from time to time.

Values are part of the lifeline that we can tug on to pull ourselves up.

Having open conversations that explore and expand the definitions we are using, add power and strength to our commitment to keep those values at the forefront of our behaviors. Sharing this discovery and development with others provides a good measure of accountability as the distractions of modern living and the fatigue associated with them pull us away from our chosen paths.

> *"Intrinsic security doesn't come from what other people think of us or how they treat us. It doesn't come from our circumstance or our position. It comes from within. It comes from inside-out congruence, from living a life of integrity in which our daily habits reflect our deepest values."*
>
> ~ Stephen Covey

EXERCISE FOR VALUES:

1. Seek out a few "Values" lists. There are plenty out there and we have included one in this chapter. Read through the list once and then go back and select what you identify as your top 20.
2. Put the list aside and review your top 20 again in a few days. Now select your top 10—the ones that when you are fully congruent and living into without thinking bring you inner peace, satisfaction, and joy. These values will probably be reflected in an experience of life as being challenging yet exciting

and fulfilling, with a significant level of ease and enjoyment.

3. Write these 10 values on a small card, laminate it, and carry it around with you daily.
4. Make time over the next few weeks to expand each value with a precise definition and a single sentence on how you are "being" that value in daily life. Keep it simple. Do one value per day.
5. Notice how you choose actions each day that are either consciously in alignment with these values, or mindlessly not.
6. Share your values with someone who knows you well and find out what they have identified as values for themselves. With loving kindness, you can be accountability partners for each other around remaining congruent with these stated qualities.

VALUES:
guideposts by which we set our course in life

VALUES LIST

As mentioned above, there are a huge range of values lists out there. Some have as many as four hundred attributes to choose from; others have as few as twenty or thirty. The following is a middle-ground compilation, with one hundred of some of the most frequently selected values. The primary purpose of these words is to give language to those qualities that reflect your innermost important characteristics for authentic living and interaction with others; this awareness

Accountability
Adventure
Authenticity
Authority
Awareness
Balance
Beauty
Boldness
Bravery
Calm
Compassion
Commitment
Competency
Confidence
Connection
Cooperation
Courage
Creativity
Community
Curiosity
Decisiveness
Dependability
Determination
Dignity
Diligence
Discipline
Discovery
Diversity
Duty
Education
Empathy
Excellence
Experience
Exploration
Fairness
Faith
Flexibility
Focus
Freedom
Friendship
Fun
Generosity
Gratitude
Growth
Happiness
Health
Honesty
Hopefulness
Humility
Humor
Imagination
Inclusion
Influence
Integrity
Intellectual Stimulation
Intimacy
Justice
Kindness
Knowledge
Leadership
Learning
Liberty
Love
Loyalty
Mindfulness
Moderation
Moral Standards
Motivation
Openness
Optimism
Organization
Passion
Peace
Power
Reason
Recognition
Resilience
Respect
Responsibility
Sacrifice
Security
Sensitivity
Sincerity
Spirituality
Stability
Status
Strength
Structure
Support
Sympathy
Teamwork
Thoughtfulness
Timeliness
Trust
Understanding
Uniqueness
Usefulness
Variety
Virtue
Vision
Wealth
Wisdom

in turn creates congruence and allows for the highest levels of sharing your individual gifts and talents with the world.

These qualities are unique for each of us, so if a value you hold dear is not listed here, write it in for yourself. And have fun!

FURTHER EXPLORATION:

Once you have chosen your top 10 values, select the 5 that most closely represent those qualities you would consider essential to your core.

1. Write down 2 or 3 actions that demonstrate what living into those values fully looks like.
2. Reflect on whether or not this is actually how you show up each day.
3. Be mindful of where, when and with whom you may find it challenging to remain congruent with what you have identified as your core values. These examples are what are known as "value conflicts."

The experience of happiness in life comes when there is complete and consistent alignment in our thoughts, actions, words, and interactions with others. Much of modern living presents patterns of distraction that move us into unconscious living where subtle (or not so subtle) feelings of discontent, unhappiness, or confusion may arise. Keeping a handy list of your values for review is one way to reinforce your own commitment to authentic living and increase the feelings of satisfaction and success from within. These states of being are intricately connected to both our mental and physical wellbeing. The ripple effect of this congruency moving out into our families, communities, and the world at large is a game-changer, capable of altering the trajectory of human beings and the planet we share.

Whenever we feel "stuck" in our outer world of work, relationships, and/or goals, it is usually because of something being stuck inside. Clarity around our values and how we are living into them can shine light on places where the readjustment of behavior or thought patterns may need to occur. This discovery process is known as mindset mastery, and while there are many paths that intersect with it they all begin with clarity.

DISCOVERING CLARITY THROUGH CURIOSITY

Mark's Nut Shop Adventure

(*a true story shared by Mark Dockendorff*)

I find that curiosity is one of the best tools to help navigate the sometimes confusing but always interesting turns in life. In fact, I have always been able to look back upon the most challenging times and identify how curiosity led me through them to greater clarity and personal growth. None was more interesting, however, than when I owned a nut shop in California.

Taking on this entrepreneurial role brought me face-to-face with a reality very different from the one I had envisioned. The business was not what I had been led to believe it would be, and buyer's remorse was instant. It was while I was in this state of stress, and feeling a plethora of uncomfortable emotions, that I started to become more and more curious. How was I going to make decisions based on what is true and most useful for me? How could I pivot and find the best way through this new scenario, so different from what I had actually prepared for?

I am blessed with an active and creative mind, which is wonderful but also requires me to be mindful of staying grounded in the greater vision that I have for myself. After exploring many creative options and seeking professional advice about the company I now owned, I ultimately sought out meditation in order to find clarity. I was seeking to find an energetic path forward that felt congruent. The curious exploration began as I followed the stillness and the energy that meditation brought me. I had a lot of thoughts about how to turn the company around and move it forward; I also began noticing two distinct energies, one that felt proactive and had greater ease, and the other that felt heavy and limiting. Both had elements of creativity. The other great awareness I had during this expansive state came in the form of a question—namely, whether or not I would have even chosen to become an entrepreneur if I knew what I currently did.

Of course I also had the typical thoughts of self-doubt ("Is this quitting?", "Am I a failure?", et cetera) running through my head like a checklist of judgments. I knew that these judgments are normal in our culture; I also knew that for many people they become the mindset from which they make their decisions—it is a mindset of ego, concern for reputation, limitation, and finite thinking. Thanks to my meditation practice—and perhaps some luck—I saw the trap and was able to avoid it. I didn't know what came next, but I knew that continuing on this path with this nut shop was definitely not it. Shortly thereafter I sold the business with full disclosure to the new owners around what this opportunity held, and what it did not.

The following quote describes how wide-open curiosity led me through this part of my journey to arrive at my decision and move onward into the unknown.

"There is no way to happiness. Happiness is the way."
~ Thich Nhat Hanh

Through reflection, I am reminded how beneficial deep inner listening is to the process of curiosity and how connected this is to finding clarity. This means paying attention to all the goings-on in the world around me through the filter of the actual relevance to my own core values, and being willing to see things differently. I came to understand that knowing is greater than blind hope and wishful thinking, and that the best knowing comes from within. When we listen with a curious mind, a mind that can engage with the infinite, we can move through the uncertainty of outer circumstances to truly live a more inspired life. ~ MJD

"Ten times a day something happens to me like this—some strengthening throb of amazement—some good sweet empathic ping and swell. This is the first, the wildest and the wisest thing I know: that the soul exists and is built entirely out of attentiveness."
~ Mary Oliver

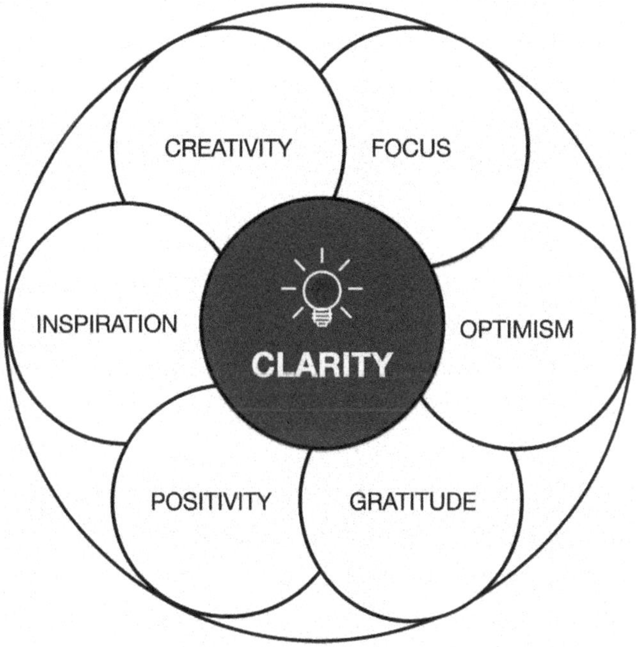

CLARITY BUBBLE

The qualities in the Bubbles such as the one above help us in the process of fine-tuning perceptions, evaluating options, and then choosing in ways that align with our True Soul. They are also character aspects that get reinforced and strengthened as we give attention to developing them. As you can see, we have included focus among the attributes we have chosen to connect with the resource of clarity. Focus is the "attentiveness" that Mary Oliver hails in so many of her poems. It is the awareness of what is, so that we can imagine what we might want.

Let's explore.

FOCUS: In physics, a focus is **"a point at which rays of light, heat, or other radiation meet after being refracted or reflected."** One can imagine the power that such a concentration of energy would generate. Harnessing that power would enable all sorts of endeavors.

In relation to ourselves, focus is defined as "a thing or place that is of greatest importance to an activity or interest." The aspect of "great importance" speaks to the transformation that occurs when we have a concentration, or meeting, of thoughts, emotions, and information that generates energy for movement within our lives.

Tools like meditation, mindfulness training, and quieting the mind all sharpen our ability to shut out external noise and hone in so we can meet the distractions of the day with strength and conviction. It is helpful to start small, with five minutes of quiet focus on a single thought or item, and slowly move up to longer periods of concentration. Being able to find that quiet at will is key to remaining grounded and calm in the midst of the scattered energies of crisis.

For those of us who are more kinesthetically oriented, there are moving meditations that can also take us to that place of internal calm. Be sure to check the resource list at the end of the book for referrals.

OPTIMISM: From the Latin *optimum,* or "best thing."

Optimism is an attitude. It encompasses the belief that the outcome of some specific endeavor will be positive, favorable, and desirable. It is helpful to have a specific outcome or result in mind in order to generate optimism about what actually occurs. Those of us labeled "eternal optimists" are able to embrace ANY outcome as having positive qualities to be learned from and appreciated. In that state of appreciation, we tend to view all things as contributing to an optimistic viewpoint on the world. In considering the dictum of assessing the glass as half full or half empty, we like to be in gratitude simply for having a glass at all!

Winston Churchill once said, "A pessimist sees the difficulty in every opportunity; an optimist sees the opportunity in every difficulty." That slight but significant shift in perspective allows for greater creativity when problem-solving, more peace when in the midst of chaos and higher levels of satisfaction with life.

Research into the effects of optimism have shown that those with an optimistic outlook on life generally experience better management of pain, better immune function, and overall greater physical function. Being optimistic lets us broaden our perception of events and engage challenges with more resilience and produce better outcomes.

Developing our levels of optimism helps us challenge our perceptions whenever we find ourselves giving audience to the "worst case scenarios" in our own thoughts. Consciously turning those thoughts around to answer the question of "What's the best possible outcome of this situation?" can start to bring our other potential options to light.

Another way to shift darker thoughts around a situation or event is to confront them with the question, "What's a better thought about this?" followed by, "What would be even better than that?!"

Retraining our thinking patterns takes time, but it is completely do-able.

GRATITUDE: This is another skill that can be trained and developed by bringing attention to the feelings it represents. The expression of thankfulness and appreciation for experiences, words, deeds of others, and beneficial associations with various elements in our lives builds this emotional muscle. I call it a muscle because it is one of the most reliable assets to call upon when life is challenging or chaotic. It can be trained, like a muscle, to be strong enough to lift us up when events seek to push us down. Gratitude has been shown to increase our resilience to difficulty, even with events that elicit elements of PTSD.

One chilly December evening a few years ago, we were wrapping holiday gifts when our house caught fire. The flames burned rapidly through a hall closet and the roof, leaving us virtually homeless and without the usual supplies for Yule time frivolity. Being immediately grateful for the safe escape of our three pets, ourselves, and a few heirlooms eased some of the trauma of having to reorient our lives midwinter. Letting go of the pain of loss to embrace the gifts of life, good friends who housed us for a few months, and the food gifts that generously came in allowed for emotional openness to occur. We embraced appreciating the beauty of the winter landscape all around us and the community abundance we were undeniably connected to.

Going into gratitude for what we DID have brought us to even deeper levels of compassion for others who experience traumatic events. It inspired us to connect with organizations and individuals who may need support for the unseen emotional processes of moving through such events. It has allowed for transformation of trauma into opportunity for growth and service to others. Most importantly, it has created in me the resilience to stay in joy and gratitude, rather than falling in to fight-or-flight responses when sensory triggers might present themselves. And for that I am also grateful.

POSITIVITY: Most of the definitions of positivity use the word "positive" in their descriptor. I usually seek to find an expansion of the concept behind the word to define it, and so I define positivity as the utilization of various human strengths and virtues in such a way as to enhance the experience of life.

Positivity is also defined as "the practice of being optimistic in attitude." Top researchers in the field of positive psychology have identified ten major forms of positivity. In the order of their relative frequency these are love, joy, gratitude, interest, hope, pride, amusement, inspiration, serenity, and awe.

Rather than getting stuck on the specific way in which you or I may define each word, ask yourself some key questions around them. These inquiries will assist you in moving away from a one-size-fits-all approach to positivity and allow your own most relevant experiences to shape how you identify and then develop this trait for yourself. Be sure to give some measure of grace to those around you to do the same.

These questions are:

- When was the last time I felt this feeling? Where was I? What was I doing?
- What else gives me that same feeling? What can I do to cultivate that feeling?
- What other triggers brings that feeling on for me?

Setting your awareness to begin noticing these ten states of positivity can actually begin to increase their prevalence in your life. Give it a try and see what happens!

INSPIRATION: the process of being mentally stimulated to do or feel something, especially to do something creative.

While many definitions of inspiration speak to the process, it is also important to take notice of the externals that trigger that process. Where do you find inspiration? In what places, with what people, and during which activities does "inspiration" flow to you?

Capturing that input honors it and begins to allow for more engagement with the aspect of creativity that accompanies inspiration. A small notebook or the "notes" feature on our smartphones is one way to begin to record the moments and encourage them to blossom into something larger.

The recognition of the process is one way of answering the call of the Divine, whatever you may identify that Energy as. Finding the courage to step into the actions that inspiration seeds in us is another layer to begin exploring on your Journey. The fun is in seeing where it takes you.

CREATIVITY: the ability to transcend traditional ideas, rules, patterns, relationships, or the like, and to create meaningful new ideas, forms, methods, interpretations. It includes the attributes of inventiveness, imagination, and ingenuity.

"The power of imagination makes us infinite."
~ John Muir

So many of the words around the central concept of Clarity are connected to one another, not only through their definitions, but through the support they offer with regard to our development and ability to live into them.

The two key words that stand out in this definition of creativity are "transcend" and "new." Creativity is being able to take inspiration in and bring forth something new that transcends the current reality and provides value that moves it forward. This quality is certainly in high demand in these times of deconstructing paradigms that no longer seem to serve the greater good and advancement of humanity and the planet.

It is from the resulting place of Clarity that we find the discernment to choose what path to follow, what gear to bring, and in what directions to pivot and turn towards. It can feel scary at times, but is also exciting and essential to our continued progress as a species.

"Courage is the measure of our heartfelt
participation with life, with another,
with a community, a work, a future.
To be courageous, is not necessarily to go
anywhere or do anything except to make
conscious those things we already
feel deeply and then to live through
the unending vulnerabilities
of those consequences."
~ David Whyte

Chapter Four

Courage

COURAGE: *the confidence to act in accordance with one's beliefs; it is the state or quality of mind or spirit that enables one to face danger, fear, or vicissitudes with self-possession, confidence, and resolution*

"In modern living most of us no longer have to worry about wild animals chasing us or severe weather eliminating our food sources or destroying our homes." I wrote those words in the middle of 2020, before the longest hurricane season in history tore through the Gulf Coast states of the U.S.; before wildfires raged unabated for months in the coastal West and Mountain states; and before epic heat in the middle of the country created a dry season that caused watering holes to disappear for livestock and crops to wither before harvest was possible.

These dramatic and extremely challenging circumstances have indeed required a new relationship to the dynamics of change. It is asking all of us to reassess where we obtain our sense of security and how we might reframe disruptions to that security as opportunities.

Crucial to this assessment is our groundedness in our personal values (i.e. clarity), so that as we face choices for reconstruction we can do so from a place of integrated awareness of a new, broader perspective. Engaging with the "adventurous and exciting" in ways that produce sustainable outcomes requires a capacity for big picture thinking, not just the immediate reflex thinking we may have a tendency to default to.

The first two stages of our Infinite Journey path are typically fairly easy to travel on. The exercises of curiosity and clarity creation are fun and engaging. Identifying components of those skillsets and bringing them into our repertoire involves a certain amount of safe mental gymnastics that is not dramatically disruptive to our lives. There is a graceful ease of implementation that can be achieved as one explores and identifies various qualities to enhance for oneself.

It becomes a test of character, however, when it comes around to stepping into actions that may be dramatically different from our previous patterns of behavior. It is while in the process of developing clarity that we begin to feel uncomfortable with paradigms that are not helping us move in the direction we have chosen to head. We begin to recognize the inner feelings of unrest and disquiet that ask us to make new choices. As we ground our personal values into our psyche, accepting circumstances or people or structures that are out of alignment with those values becomes unpleasant and unproductive. Learning to recognize those feelings as indicators of areas that need evaluation is one of the next skillsets to develop.

When learning to discern true danger from emotional imaginations of danger it can be of great benefit to return to the inquiry process. Here are some of the questions we coaches often pose to clients when we perceive timidity around action is entering their strategic thinking.

1. The classic: "What's the worst that could happen?" and "How likely is that to actually happen?"
2. "What about this scenario do you find challenging?"—or, its cousin—"What scares you about that?" Simply giving our concerns a name can reduce the charge our emotions have given to elements of the unknown. It also allows us to bring in what we DO know about a challenging situation and its potential solutions.
3. "What are you tolerating?" and "What is that keeping you from having/enjoying at this time?"
4. "What other choices can you make in this situation that feel easier/safer/more predictable?"
5. "What one choice feels like a bit of stretch but do-able?"
6. "What would make this effort more fun?"
7. "What do you need to keep moving forward?" and "What is stopping you from moving forward?"

Allowing one's imagination free reign to express itself is often an end solution to the dilemma. One process—the expressing out loud of unlikely scenarios—is brilliant for identifying our influence over them and strengthening our confidence to exert such influence. As you will see in the Courage Bubble diagram, confidence is included for its role in reinforcing the will to step into action and stay there.

> *"There is no desire that gets fulfilled without courage. No hope that produces results without action."* ~ (from a lecture delivered by Moira in 2010 to an all-women entrepreneurs' business development group)

COURAGE BUBBLE

Take a moment to reflect upon how you may be either living into or avoiding these qualities associated with COURAGE.

ACTION: This one is fairly self-explanatory.

When you have an idea or a change you wish to engage with, how energetically do you "step into action" for making it happen? Do you carefully outline steps that will move you ever closer towards achieving it? Or do you slip into "paralysis by analysis" and spend more time evaluating options rather than choosing one? Do you get stuck in the inertia of being afraid of making a wrong choice, or are you willing to learn whatever you may need to from any choice, knowing you can always choose again?

What is your understanding of the concept that "No choice is a choice"?

Where do you go or who do you turn to for support when faced with the sometimes difficult task of "choosing"? Make a list of your resources in this area, and if there are fewer than three give some thought to how you might grow it. Keep in mind, though, that these are merely sources of reflection, not judgment, for evaluating the various factors that may be involved in stepping into action.

Know too that this resource list is not restricted to people. For example, I find a long hike in the outdoors to be my best source of reflection. When I find myself stuck in a decision-making process it is often because I have spent more time indoors at the computer than out on the trail. As soon as I rebalance that for myself, solutions flow. Action fuels action.

COMMITMENT: The exercises in the previous section around Clarity support the aspect of commitment one is able to bring to any endeavor. In this area we often ask clients to rank their degree of commitment using a scale of 1 to 10, with 1 being "I don't really care at all about this project or issue" and 10 being "I am fully and deeply connected to the energy of getting this project done." This number can apply to how we feel about a relationship, a purchase, or a move or choice of any kind. Determining where our emotions land along that scale helps us gain clarity around how we might raise our level of commitment, or whether to step away from the option at hand and make a different choice altogether.

Commitment speaks to levels of resolve, dedication, and attentiveness to the issue at hand. The higher our level of commitment to anything, the higher the likelihood of fulfilling on the promise of the proposition, whatever it may be.

BOLDNESS: In a historical context, this quality sometimes evokes images of wildly screaming clansmen brandishing swords as they run down a hill at the enemy at dawn. In our modern, everyday lives, it can be as simple as saying good morning to a stranger, exuberantly expressing our joy at good news with a coworker, or speaking our convictions with grace and firmness to one who has a different perspective.

Do some freeform expressive writing about what the word boldness evokes for you, then reflect on whether this is a state of being you could imagine yourself engaging in. If not, then spend some time looking up definitions of the word, and profiles of some people who have been described as "bold."

Share some of these discoveries with a good friend and explore the concept together. In the midst of this process you *will* find alignment with some definition that you can then use to evaluate how you are showing up in your life when things get challenging. It will also show you how boldness might be employed to support actions you may want to take.

CONFIDENCE: This quality is one which gets reinforced as we step into courage. It is a self-generating emotion that comes from stepping into action, creating results, staying committed to our chosen course of action and, through boldness, discovering that what doesn't kill us makes us stronger. If we apply our clarity of values to the actions we choose, confidence will ensue as we receive feedback through success or adjustment for what might come next.

The feedback loop that the qualities connected to courage bring us supports the definition of confidence as "a feeling of self-assurance arising from one's appreciation of one's own abilities or qualities." As Mark says, "Knowing I am being congruent with my core values and authentic in my language and actions gives me confidence that I am going to be in joy (enjoy) with whatever I am delivering."

Think of a time when you had an unshakeable level of confidence in a choice you made or an action you took. What were the factors that contributed to that feeling? Who else might have been a witness to that confidence and could give you input on how you showed up?

Confidence comes from the Latin word *fidere,* which means "to trust." If you feel as if you are lacking in this trust, take whatever negative self-talk may be instilling doubt within yourself and ask the reverse question about the issue. For example, if you feel you can't do something, ask yourself what it might be like if you could. What beneficial change would show up in your life? What would you experience or enjoy? Painting an inner picture of possibility can fuel the confidence necessary to begin taking action.

DARING is a word closely associated with confidence and often seen as a synonym for boldness, as it too is comprised of a sense of adventure, fearlessness, and a certain measure of audacity as one steps into action. The distinction, though, is that daring embodies a spirit of dynamism; it requires more willingness to explore the unknown. Teddy Roosevelt's oft-quoted "Man in the Arena" speech, delivered in 1910, applauds the aspect of the individual who dares greatly, regardless of outcome. It's worth looking up.

How willing are you to try new approaches to challenges when the outcome is uncertain. How willing are you to fall on your face in the trying, pick yourself up, and push on? What factors need to be in place for you to do so. Are there a lot of these factors, or just a few.

Consider how much flexibility you have in this arena of adventurousness? What might you do to step outside of your current comfort zone and try something completely new and different? Meet someone completely different from your usual circle of acquaintances? If you get stuck for ideas, ask someone who knows you well what they might consider "daring" for you to try? Journal around how it makes you feel to simply contemplate this.

If you do choose to engage in the suggestion, journal about how you felt during and afterwards. Be sure to acknowledge your courage in doing so.

HOPE: This quality is the fuel for the energies of several of the others in the Courage Bubble. It is defined as a feeling of confident expectation in an outcome that persists through unknown components that are yet to unfold within a process. Hope is distinct from wishful thinking in that it is linked to grounded knowledge about an issue which builds trust in the steps being implemented to achieve an outcome. Hope connects one with the character strength of discernment. This skill assists with the creation of effective action plans and is a dynamic resource of courage.

Whenever feelings of hopelessness descend there is *always* some measure of action we can take to shift them. For example, any activity that involves physical engagement, whether it's walking around the block or simply moving in place, takes us back into the realm of positive emotions. When we can recreate a daily ratio of three or four positive emotional moments to every neutral or negative one, we begin to experience more steady states of hope and optimism.

Take some time to identify the key positive emotions you experience within the course of a single day. Make a note of how frequently you experience them and how long you "stay in the glow."

These positive emotions include feelings such as awe, wonder, thankfulness, joy, curiosity, happiness, laughter, peacefulness, and love.

Begin to take notice of these emotions for a full week and reflect on how it impacts the aspect of hope you find yourself bringing to various challenges in your life. Track this for a full month and see what changes!

JOURNEY INTO COURAGE

A Coaching Story

I would describe my mental/emotional state before learning some of these principles as wildly ambitious, uncomfortably unsure, and ultimately insecure. These emotional aspects were reflecting in the management of my business, in my participation in my marriage, and also in my friendships and relationships.

With my business, there was the fear that my team would realize how overwhelmed I felt in trying to generate more revenue for our company while at the same time trying to guide them to a new height of operational excellence. Similarly, with my home life, the challenge was how to fulfill my wife's need for stability, security, and leadership from her husband while I quietly wrestled with redefining my ideas of manhood (in my mid-thirties). Beyond those primary relationships, this inner journey of reflection manifested in general encounters with friends, colleagues, and even family as a "hiding." It became a game of receiving their accolades for my accomplishments as a business owner, devoted husband, and consistent leader while shielding them from the idea that I felt challenged or uncomfortable with the quality of my execution of those roles.

My main concerns were failure and exposure. I was not thriving in the roles I had achieved or the positions that I had maintained as a professional, husband, or leader. There was a stifling weight of supporting the exaggerated ideals of my success while consciously and anxiously hiding behind those facades so that my audience could not see how feverishly I was struggling to figure it all out. From all of that arose a palpable F.O.M.U.—or the fear of messing up.

Seeking out and speaking with a coach first gave me a sense of "peace in my storms" because she ALWAYS had a simple remedy. That taught me that the solutions I was seeking were simple and apparently just outside of my perspective. Our coaching conversations gave me an alternative vantage point to reach for whenever I felt stuck.

Shifts for me came as I embraced the exercise of reframing my perspectives. The statements that I was making to myself about myself were often couched in my mind's worst-case scenario. Those negative projections never had the certainty of truth that I was ascribing to them, and any future consequences that I was hoping to avoid would not have been as damning as I had imagined them. The key was learning to reframe my perspective to recognize the positive aspects and opportunities of the present day. The opportunity of "today" began to have more emotional priority than the potential perils of future failures or a diminished public perception.

The new mindset that emerged was one of remaining positive and present versus being negative and projecting.

That perspective became the foundation for a courage that I had long sought. That courage manifested in the ideas of forgiveness, transparency, emotional articulation, and diligent action. My courage began with relieving myself of the pressure of my own expectations. My courage today is found in expressing to myself, to my coaches, to my wife, and to the world when I am not okay, if that is indeed my truth at the moment. My courage extends as I can articulate to myself what I want, and what the simplest, most efficient steps in that direction are. As I am able to stave off distraction and make those few steps my priority, my courage produces the things I seek or sometimes other outcomes that are even greater than what I had imagined.

The effort is ongoing, and as I continually reframe my perspective so that I have a foundation of truth and positivity to work from, I continue to find the progress that I am seeking.

Over the series of our conversations, I have developed a "what would Dr. Forsythe say" space in my own mind that helps to challenge my approach in the moments when my inputs are not yielding my desired outcomes. The shift for me has been to understand that if I just change the way I am thinking about a situation, I am more likely to change the way I am participating in it. And that changes everything.
~ Jason Greenfield, Owner/CEO at The Greenfield Group, Corp. and Greener Fields Wellness, Dallas, TX

A fish cannot drown in water.
A bird does not fall in air.
Each creature God made
Must live in its own true nature.
~ 13th century mystic
Mechthild of Magdeburg

Chapter Five

Congruence

CONGRUENCE: *a state of harmony*

Congruence is a term used by Carl Rogers (a humanistic psychologist) to ***describe a state in which a person's ideal self and actual experience are consistent or very similar.***

In psychology and neurolinguistic programming (NLP), congruence could be ***defined as a rapport with oneself,*** *or* ***internal and external consistency, perceived by others as sincerity or certainty.***

Of all the themes we have been exploring here, congruence has proven to be the most slippery to define. The closest word we have to express the meaning is "alignment"—when aspects and qualities within a process align harmoniously with one another and begin to create a well-blended result, that is congruence.

Several other synonyms—harmony, compatibility, consistency, and balance—showed up to expand the understanding of what this concept entails. After hours of working together to bring clarity to our description of this concept, Mark and I realized that more than any of the others it was truly grounded in mastering emotional intelligence. That is the key to comprehending how to create congruence, how to recognize it, how to maintain it, and how to know when we are slipping away from it.

Mark spoke repeatedly about "gut feelings" as barometers for determining whether one's experiences are congruent with their core values, while I deferred to intuition as the guidance system that notifies us of challenges to this state. Recognizing internal discomfort as an indicator that our congruence has been diminished, lessened, or even made absent by choices and reactions to external stimuli can be a challenge. Most of us don't want to look at discomfort or "gut feeling" for the learning that it presents, much less put energy into moving through it to get to those wisdom gems. To do so requires courage.

Whatever we call them, such feelings are always a signal to stop, refocus, regroup, evaluate, and then choose. Sometimes they're an indication that our current mindset is no longer helping us to move us forward in alliance with what we have identified as our soul purpose. The core values we've spent time exploring and identifying become points of reflection for analyzing our feelings. Refocusing our attentions on those values, and returning to a state of non-judgmental curiosity, helps us discover where the incongruency may be and allows us the opportunity to realign with that state of harmony.

The words we chose to include in our Bubble of Congruence reflect what one might experience when they are living into congruence with their thoughts and actions. A key commonality among these qualities is the ease they bring to our life's experiences.

When we are in congruence it becomes easier to recognize collaborative opportunities that will serve to further a cause or project. It feels easier to access the skills that define resiliency during challenging times. Joy and serenity are present without striving to create them. Our default state of being is clearly identifiable as authentic and connected to all in graceful ways.

Throughout this book we have been discussing how we can transition to what is useful when new, often challenging situations arise. This becomes our default response when we move along the path of life in a state of congruence with our truest nature. Learning how to stay in alignment with our core essence means re-examining core values on a regular basis. What researchers have found is that the importance of values can shift and vary as we move through various phases of maturity. Some of us will argue that the genuine truth of our core essence does not change over time, it only deepens or gets ignored based on the level of consciousness we bring to life choices.

MOVING THROUGH CHALLENGE TO FIND CONGRUENCE

A Story of Triumph over Trials

As we gathered stories from clients we have worked with, we were fortunate to also connect with other coaches willing to share their own personal stories of transformation. Here is one of those.

Zan Marshall Ray is an entrepreneurial pioneer who took her experiences of self-discovery, hard work, curiosity, and intuition and molded them into a successful business coaching platform she and her partner now share nationally and internationally.

She is quick to credit her humble roots from a farm outside Memphis, Tennessee as instrumental in building the work ethic she called upon to sustain herself when life got tough. The industry she was trained in was one filled with negative influences and distractions, and might have pulled her completely off track were it not for her inner knowing that she was truly destined for something greater. Trusting that inner sense allowed her to remain curious about "what else is possible," even as limitations brought on by social pressures and peer influences took her down the destructive tract of alcohol and substance abuse.

Recognizing the incongruence of these social influences with her core values gave Zan the courage to see that these behaviors were actually covering up her authentic self. It was not until she reached what she refers to as "rock bottom" that she reached out to some colleagues who had offered her some alternatives to consider. When she finally accepted their offers, and embraced her own need for support, she began to learn a new way of living into the beauty of the world and the gifts she embodied.

Zan was always aware of possessing a strong intuitive sense about the core of others and had used this skill to mentor and support them to levels of success within her industry. Now, as she moved away from the negative influences and numbing behaviors, she realized how much of her own potential she had not tapped into. Learning to take better care of herself produced better results for her own business ventures as well as for those she mentored.

Zan became clear about the value of surrounding oneself with positive influences and supportive players in sustaining the high levels of performance she had come to expect of herself and others. She used this clarity to set clear boundaries within the confines of her business, and to realize even higher levels of expanded awareness. She had always reinvented herself through the rebuilding of her business brands when challenges arose; now, however, she began to rebuild from a newfound place of inner personal power. She began to recognize that many of the strategies for success that she could bring to others were also connected to the mindset work that coaching offers. As she got clear about her life's purpose she established a personal Code of Conduct by which she measures her actions: "To be a guiding light for others" and "to be a love and happiness magnet." The Power Virtues she lives into include several of the resource qualities we have expanded on in this book: Courage, Faith, Determination, and Love.

Today, Zan's company, Elevating My Business, is a premier coaching firm that supports salons and small business enterprises nationwide in elevating revenues and creating sustainable and fulfilling ventures. She is a sought-after speaker at conferences and expos nationwide, where she shares the strategies she has developed in collaboration with partner Tom Collins.

Zan is the first to say that she is still learning and peeling back the layers of discovery to find out what's next. Her professional calling as a coach and business mentor allows her to share her journey with others and support them in the constructive ways she so dearly appreciates.

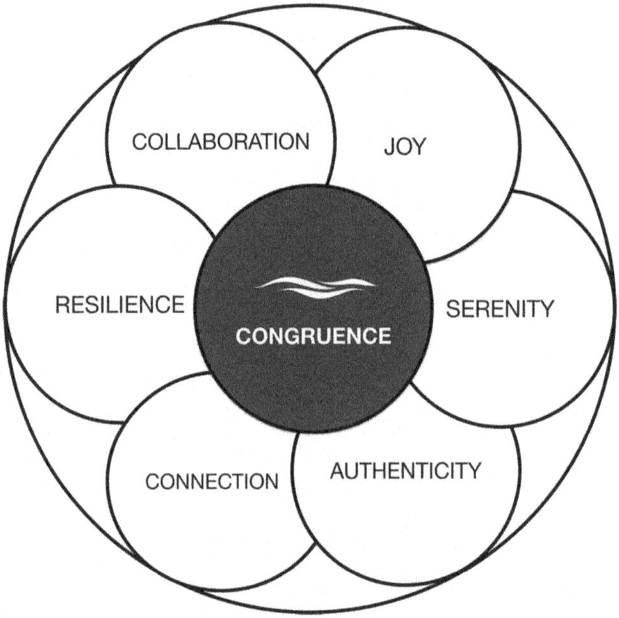

CONGRUENCE BUBBLE

BEING CONGRUENT WITH OUR VALUES

Recall the list of ten values that you identified for yourself in the chapter on Clarity. You will probably retain most of them throughout your life, perhaps rearranging their order of significance as circumstances bring on different levels of energetic engagement over time. Reexamining our values from time to time gives us the opportunity to look at whether our commitment to a particular value is still moving us toward our deepest fulfillment of purpose for the short time we are in this physical world.

This review process also reveals when we have slid into a state of complacency, doing what feels easy rather than what is required in order to remain true to ourselves. One indicator that the values you have chosen for yourself are connected to that deeper Inner True Self is the degree of excitement you feel when you read them again.

An interesting way to discover how congruent you are in your current state of being is to have someone you trust, and, who knows you fairly well, to choose the top ten values they feel you live into from the bigger list. Do not share your list of chosen values with them until after they have done this, as their selections will tell you how authentically your actions are demonstrating to the world what you believe in. You can then ask the person how you might show up more in alignment with your desired values, compared to how you are currently doing so in their eyes.

You could also do this exercise with someone who only knows you casually and thus can offer a more objective perspective on your behaviors.

Keep in mind that we humans are "meaning-making machines," and the background from which someone assigns meanings to the words on a values list can influence how they choose them. Be sure to keep a level of openness to the conversation, and perhaps a dictionary handy, to be able to establish good clarity in the sharing. Ultimately the measure of the veracity of our choices is whether they register as "true north" on our internal compass, as this is what will stimulate movement towards congruency.

"Caring for myself is not self-indulgence,
it is self-preservation, and that is
an act of political warfare."
~ Audre Lorde

Chapter Six

Self-Care

SELF-CARE: *The practice of taking an active role in protecting one's own well-being and happiness, particularly during periods of stress*

Evaluating our level of congruence and then taking on some of the exercises to increase it can be an emotionally demanding and even anxiety-producing task. This brings to mind the topic of self-care and the practices that most resonate with us, both on a regular basis and when we are feeling challenged.

SELF-CARE IN TIMES OF CHANGE

All of the ideas we have put forth are powerful in creating a foundation for balance when the road gets rocky or obstacles appear along the way. Oftentimes, simply stepping back in observation is all that is needed to restore one's fortitude and perseverance. This is just a fancy way of talking about "self-care."

Too often we relegate self-care to the bottom of our lists of things to do or pay attention to. I often remind clients that when we travel by plane, we are instructed that should a situation requiring oxygen masks arise we should put on our own mask first before assisting another. The everyday wisdom in this is not to be ignored, as it applies to many other circumstances where we are asked to step up and be of service to others.

Recognizing our own state of reserves and the needs for restoration is not a sign of weakness, but one of incredible wisdom. Yet we find caregivers—and many of the rest of us in this time of global challenges—dismissing the value of taking time for that process. The result is the creation of states of depletion so destructive that we can no longer function optimally.

Self-care is not a luxury; it is an essential element of productive living. Shifting into this mindset can be done in gentle ways that increase the success of developing consistent practices. That said, changing our behaviors, while exciting in the best of times, is also inherently challenging. We must give ourselves the grace of time, not only to see results but to have the changes become steady habits that we access with regularity and ease.

An acronym that comes to mind using the word CARE is *Creating Awareness for Restoring Energy*. I tell clients who are servant leaders and involved in dozens of projects at the cost of their own well-being that "You can't pour from an empty cup." A search for this phrase will turn up lots of suggestions on increasing one's awareness of the importance for self-care and incorporating more of it into one's routines. We offer a few suggestions below.

> *"An empty lantern provides no light. Self-care is the fuel that allows your light to shine brightly."*
> ~ Unknown

BEGIN WITH "WHAT IS"

The first step in crafting an effective self-care routine is to simply acknowledge that you need one. Recognize your feelings of overwhelm or anxiety or frustration and own them. State them out loud in a clear way to someone in your innermost circle and if no one is there, state them out loud to yourself!

Notice where in your body you are stuffing these emotions—it will likely manifest as tension, tightness, or internal upset—and release it. How? By using the breath. Just focus on where you have noticed the tension and breathe deeply into that area with intention to let it go. This is the number one technique for enhancing healthy energy flow throughout our system. It can be done anytime, anywhere, sitting or standing, preferably two to three times a day. There are numerous videos and clips that can help you learn to regulate your breathing rhythms efficiently, instead of sliding into hyperventilation or continuing patterns of shallow breathing. Resources are listed in the resource section.

The regular check-in for what and where our body may

be holding on to energy instead of allowing unimpeded flow connects directly to the state of hormonal and emotional integrity within our systems as well.

With practice, you can retrain your brain to change unhelpful thinking patterns and in doing so ease the process of implementing healthier habits in multiple areas of life. Another term for this process is "awareness of anxiety." Oftentimes the onset of anxiety happens gradually, with continuous stressful input that builds upon itself and goes unnoticed by us until we're feeling overwhelmed. The most appropriate analogy is that of the frog sitting in a pot of water on the stove. The temperature increases so slowly that the frog doesn't realize it is being boiled until it's too late to be able to jump out. Prevention is by far preferable to the overload responses that can be necessary once this boiling point is reached. Consider adding some of the following activities into your routines, one at a time. Give yourself at least a week to ten days to judge if the activity you chose is working for you, knowing that by definition a cumulative benefit takes time to show up in a measurable way.

SELF-CARE ACTIVITIES

1. Take a break from stress-inducing input you have no control over: multiple scrolling through news reports in a single day; social media feeds on issues outside your immediate world; and comparative reviewing of the lives of strangers that instills envy or sadness that your life is not "as good" as theirs.

   If you find it difficult to shift these behaviors, start

small. Set a timer to give yourself a mandatory "vacation break" from your devices for 2-3 minutes. Do this 4 times a day at 2- to 3-hour intervals. When you take these breaks, drink a big glass of fresh water, for hydration is key to optimal heart and brain function. Use this time to engage in a stretch/breath break as well. See the resources section for places to find helpful videos.

2. Make sure you are fueling yourself adequately throughout a day's activities. Being hangry can cause mental sharpness to wane and emotional judgement to become a bit impaired, so keep on hand high-protein, complex-carbohydrate whole foods such as fruits, nuts, cheese cubes, et cetera. If it's been more than 3 hours since you consumed anything, have a snack.

3. Take a midday break to engage in 20 minutes of expressive writing. Positive psychology studies in schools with both teachers and students found that doing freeform, spontaneous writing on a daily basis for as little as 4 days in a row increased feelings of happiness and health for up to 6 weeks afterwards. Some of these feelings remained for as long as 3 months.

4. Create a gratitude journal and commit to entering 5 things each day that you are grateful for. Australian studies have shown that gratitude triggers emotional release of negative states of emotion and increases relief, calmness, and levels of spirituality. It also provides positive connection to others and expands

perspectives.

5. Moving meditation and mindfulness training is another discipline to consider exploring as these practices have been shown to lower symptoms of anxiety and depression and increase self-esteem. Moving meditation can include simply walking around one's yard for 5 minutes or taking a dance break of 4-6 minutes. Resources for these techniques can be found online and in the resources section at the end of this book.
6. In the evening, have music that is uplifting and/or classical in nature playing in the background, rather than chatter from digital sources.
7. Nature sounds, which are not the same as white noise, as a backdrop for evening meals have the effect of reducing blood pressure, lowering anxiety, and releasing tension on both physical and emotional levels. Explore.org is an excellent source of these sounds.

If you notice your anxiety causing inertia in your daily life for more than 7 days, we do encourage you to seek out support from an external source. This can be in the form of professional support, group interaction, or personal guidance from a trusted advisor.

"You should write because you love the
shape of stories and sentences and
the creation of different words on a page.
Writing comes from reading, and reading is
the finest teacher of how to write."
~ Annie Proulx

Chapter Seven

A Few More C's

LANGUAGE: *a* ***system of conventional spoken, manual (signed),*** *or* ***written symbols by means of which human beings,*** *as* ***members of a social group and participants in its culture, express*** *themselves. The functions of language include communication, the expression of identity, play, imaginative expression, and emotional release.*

Language, words, and literature have been a passion of mine since I was very young. I grew up with a father who had such a thick Caribbean accent that many of my classmates could not understand him when he spoke. I never heard him to have an accent at all.

That exposure to nuances of pronunciation and learning to "feel" into meaning when others spoke gave me an interesting skill that I only discovered when I began to travel the world. I found that I rarely had a problem understanding meaning from others, regardless of our respective languages, whether I was ordering a late-night dinner in a rural German *gästehaus* from staff that spoke no English whatsoever (and I, no German), or being able to find and pay for water while out on an early morning run in the countryside of Japan. I have always been able to create connection and exchange with light-heartedness and generosity wherever I may be. I often refer to this as "speaking human."

Early exposure to the magic of reading made me a bibliophile by the age of five or six. Sneaking off to read until dark up in the branches of our backyard willow tree or having a flashlight under the covers after my sisters had gone to sleep was *de rigueur* for my younger years. Aside from our wonder-filled multivolume Encyclopedia Britannica, my favorite "big book" was the thirty-five-pound Complete Unabridged Dictionary I moved around with well into my thirties. To this day I keep a two-volume hardback dictionary set on my bookshelf to peruse and get lost in as I marvel at the root source of words and language history and indulgently wander into the expansive world of synonyms and antonyms.

All of this leads up to how Mark and I came up with the wonderful alliterative quality of the four words we chose for the concept identifications herein. The English language has only twenty-six letters and forty basic sounds, but the infinitesimal variations of combinations makes it one of the more difficult languages to master. The "hard c" sound falls into the category of sharp vibrational resonances that grab our attention and carry an energetic of action with their use.

Softer consonant sounds and blended consonants generally instill more soothing responses and relax us when we hear them. (Think cherry, choice, cedar, circle, and so on.)

While this is a bit of a linguistic generalization, it still applies to how we chose the category terms which grabbed our attention for use. They are words which are connected to being in action around one's life and that is the energy we wished to impart to readers of this volume.

Alliteration is a literary construct often used in advertising to create a memorable impression on the end user. Many well-known brands have utilized this technique in the creation of their product names or company logos. We were simply going with terms that energized us as we discussed them. I have always been a fan of alliterative phrases.

During the selection process it emerged that several other C words easily fit into the same model of high energy, ease of use, and relevance to our topics. Rather than overuse these wonderfully alliterative words within the content, we thought it would be fun to share them here. We encourage you to contemplate how they may associate with various aspects of the categories already discussed. Enjoy!

Communication	Capable	Cooperation
Creativity	Compassion	Community
Consistency	Consideration	Collective
Character	Coherence	Calm

For some additional fun, here are a few "soft" Cs:

Choice	Change
Center	Celebrate

And lastly, but by no means least, here is one more word game to play with.

The intention of this book was to support the reader in finding effective ways to create calm in their lives even while chaos and disruptive events may be whirling around them. In reflecting on techniques used by first responders, including trained Wilderness First Responders such as myself, as well as other crisis workers, the use of acronyms helps one to stay focused on best practices in the midst of chaos. The easier we can make the remembering of principles, the more likely we are to retain the energy of the concept. Early one morning, as dawn was breaking here at 8,500 feet in the mountains where I live, and as the breezes were blowing and the birds were singing, an acronym began floating through my mind. Some might call it a mnemonic. It is connected to the letters in the word CALM.

Whatever you might choose to call it, I found it brought me immediately into the essence of how "being" calm could feel and what kind of behavior would support that state of being. Repeating the phrases inspired by the letters quickly felt like a mantra.

C - Calm	C - Compassionate
A - Awareness With	A - Action from a
L - Loving	L - Loving
M - Mindfulness	M - Mindset

I invite you to play around with creating one that has relevance for you and to use it whenever you begin to feel the tensions of chaos pulling you away from your center.

C - ________________________________

A - ________________________________

L - ________________________________

M - ________________________________

It is abundantly clear to me that if we can move forward in this world with a mindset of loving kindness, compassion, and mindfulness, what we create will be infused with the qualities of peace and calm. I know that sounds pretty good to me.

"Always leave enough time in your life to do something that makes you happy, satisfied, even joyous. Sustainability, ensuring the future of life on earth, is an infinite game, the endless expression of generosity on behalf of all."

~ Paul Hawken

*"Although the world is full of suffering,
it is also full of the overcoming of it."*
~ Helen Keller

Chapter Eight

Reflections on 2020

While gathering content for this book we reached out to many individuals for their insights around the life journeys they have been on. Not surprisingly, we found the enormity of the events of 2020 have left an indelible impression on them, as they have on all of us. We were each at a different place in the Journey when this year found us, and so we each have a different tale of engagement with the experience. Here are some of the precious sharings we received from others. It is our hope that readers can find value and wisdom to call upon as we each continue on our individual paths, with the knowing that we are all in this together. And together we are stronger than we know.

Some of the most compelling stories we heard were from solopreneurs who found themselves repeatedly thrust into agonizing choice points around the economics of small business management including rent payments, employee support, and often basic lifestyle sustainability. The courage of these individuals to seek out support when the going got tough was something we all can learn from, as was their brave quest to find clarity in creating workable solutions to the unique new challenges brought by the pandemic.

Here are just a few of the spontaneous insights of feelings and emotions shared with us.

"This year I got more vulnerable with mySELF. It was uncomfortable, frustrating, confusing, wild, intoxicating, sensual, liberating, and scary as hell. There is an energy of being receptive to what is moving, breathing, and being awakened in my soul in a gentle and heart opening way.

This year has gifted me the feeling of just being OPEN to opportunity and possibility even beyond my desires. The unfolding of the new chapter will come and there is a feeling of excitement within my bones, a knowing to trust, and a new intimate relationship with the UNKNOWN.

If you are finding yourself in the chaotic unknown let it in like a new lover, be vulnerable ... ♥...Trust In the Feel of It..." ~ *Jenna Pfingston, Primal Embodied Wisdom practitioner, Colorado*

"Week 36 in pregnancy! It's getting close and really hard at the same time. Pregnancy has triggered lots of underlying anxiety and insomnia issues for me, as well as other physical symptoms. I write this message because a lot of times on Facebook, we see image after image of happy, "perfect" people and we oftentimes compare our lives to these snapshots. The happy photos aren't fake, just as the moments of sadness, frustration, impatience, and physical pain I've been experiencing aren't fake. It's all part of the human experience. It all deserves to be shared because during times like this, people need to see a balanced view of life in all its forms and colors. You can struggle through adversity and still share the genuinely joyful moments of your life. It's not either/or. It's and." ~ *Maria Pascucci-Maciejewski, New York, professional speaker and coach, www.campuscalm.com*

"I found this year of intermittent mandatory isolations provided some spaciousness for examining many aspects of how I give to others. I have found that I can now be more stable for others and my tank is no longer completely empty. I feel as if I am calmly and steadily moving towards wholeness. This event has also pointed out for me that who we have in our lives is critical for our own health and well-being." ~ *Martha Hartney, Boulder, Colorado, lawyer, mother, Integralist*

To find even more stories of how others have navigated the process of finding ways to live simply and live well, check out the compilation book, *Sustainable Happiness* edited by Sarah Van Gelder (2014). It contains nineteen stories relating to why this is an important quest to go on, as well as some studies validating what we know about achieving happiness. The short stories share how individuals in various walks of life are incorporating the focus into their routines, at work, at home, and in life in general. There are bound to be insights of benefit for any who choose to read it.

One other category of unsung corona heroes we want to acknowledge are the stay-at-home parents of school-aged children, whether those children are six, sixteen, or twenty-six.

The overlay of uncertainty into already chaotic school schedules, disparate learning styles, and individual personal needs called for Herculean strength of time and energy management that most were completely unprepared for.

The imposition of social distancing removed the supportive connections of playdates, group outings, and field trips. Parents have found themselves isolated amidst the chaos of learning, which many previously smiled at when visiting classrooms for pick-up. Unfortunately, positive memories often dim in moments of crisis, which is what this new terrain sometimes feels like. To remember what made us chuckle at these cacophonic environments can now help us get through the lack of control that has recently become part of everyday life.

There is no "one size fits all" solution to the range of challenges being presented in various forms across the world. Access to external resources is similarly varied; however, there are internal resources that when developed and encouraged can become ingenious sources of unexpected solutions that work. Some are so basic as to be considered insignificant to suggest. We disagree with that assessment and contend that there are indeed times when simple and basic are exactly what's called for.

And so we suggest the tools of breathing, pausing, and reflecting, even for twenty seconds (sixty is even better), to allow the discord to wash over and through us and for fresh perspective to enter as we cultivate curiosity and seek clarity on next steps. Each breath in brings oxygen to our blood to enhance the processes of creative thinking; each breath out has the potential to release what no longer serves us. There are dozens of videos on YouTube around the breath practices in yoga, mindfulness, and meditation styles which can impart ideas on how to incorporate easy practices into one's daily structure. It can be helpful to include the stay-at-home students in learning the practices as well.

Being curious about the truth behind apparent chaos helps us find the clarity needed to choose a way forward that can serve ourselves and those around us. Using the breath in this way also helps us reconnect with aspects of humor and laughter that can bring additional perspectives to the moment as well.

Pausing in reflection allows us to stay in touch with the different level of intimacy and love that exists as we "school" our children. It is a quality not present in a group setting of thirty or forty youngsters, no matter how caring a teacher may be. Separating our minds from the issues of tight spaces, increased computer time, multiple conversations, mood swings and more allows us to refocus on the core values we have built around our families to begin with.

> *"We cannot love issues, but we can love people, and the love of people reveals to us the way to deal with issues."*
>
> ~ Henri J.M. Nouven, theologian

Curiosity and clarity are so closely interwoven that it is interesting to explore them separately here. Nonetheless, the process of being curious around something like the topic of values allows for progression towards clarity about how we make choices of living into them. Take time to review the values lists in the Clarity section of this book. As you move through the exercises there reflect upon how they have influenced your navigation of some of the challenges we have all experienced this past year. You may find areas in which you wish to adjust behaviors or change choices altogether.

"Your breathing is your greatest friend. Return to it in all your troubles and you will find comfort and guidance."

~ Unknown

Keeping the breath central to the process of exploring your values will create the opportunity to re-inject the qualities of play and wonder into the journey and contribute to the creation of experiences filled with more optimism.

Conscious breathing also allows us to recognize times when it is beneficial to engage in forgiveness. Accepting that we are not always strong, or always prepared, or even always capable of managing challenges, is an important first step to discovering resources that will support us. Finding the way to personal forgiveness when overwhelm or frustration enters brings additional restoration to potentially depleting circumstances.

"Never forget that to forgive yourself is to release trapped energy that could be doing good work in the world."

~ D. Patrick Miller, journalist, author

HELPING CHILDREN DEVELOP THESE SKILLS

The world is a dynamic, often chaotic place to be. Today's ease of connectivity brings global events to our fingertips, regardless of their physical distance from us. Moreover, responses to events in other areas can bring the underlying issues of conflict and turmoil right to our front door. Children are being asked daily to process this range of disruptive information with very little filtration of its meaning or relevance to their own lives.

As adults we are mandated with guiding and leading these younger members of our society towards healthy functioning with one another. It is helpful if we have already undertaken that task for ourselves so that we can speak firsthand as to what is successful. As we master the skillsets put forth in this book, those qualities of calm reflection and mindfulness, we begin to model what is possible for those looking to us for validation.

Children have an amazing capacity to engage easily with many of the attributes we have spoken about and are often our best teachers when it comes to possessing unjaded enthusiasm for trying something new. Their naturally high levels of curiosity allow them to embrace some of the fundamental aspects of courage and exploration that adults find challenging. It is the task of adults to encourage the retention of those levels and to continue to nurture the connection to clarity, courage, and coherence that it can produce.

By continuing to deepen our own levels with some of the suggested exercises, we can become adept at recognizing those areas of reinforcement needed by young people. We can also begin to support the progression into the other concepts in ways that strengthen overall resilience and creativity.

FROM THE MOUTH OF BABES

A great example of how this manifests was shown to me as I was in the process of writing this book.

Earlier this year I had suggested to my then six-year-old grandson to join me in my nightly ritual of gratitude expression. I typically state out loud five things I am grateful for from the day. I use the five fingers on one hand to count them down and always end up using both hands or more as the recognition to the abundance I enjoy expands. I find it to be a wonderful way to unwind from the mental chatter of the day and fall into deep, restorative sleep.

The first time we tried this exercise together at the end of a busy day, I suggested he simply state three things he was thankful for. I gave him the option of choosing three things he was happy to have done during the day or three people he felt happy about having in his life, or anything that came to mind. He was uncomfortable at first and struggled to find three things that were "the right answer." We worked on his letting go of any judgment about right or wrong (grandmas are great at supporting that).

For the next few months, whenever we had a sleepover, I did this exercise at the close of storytime.

Several months later, he, now seven, and his five-year-old sister were once again snuggling down with me in preparation for sleep. When I suggested gratitude time, they could barely contain themselves enough to allow each other, or me, to contribute. I had to ask each of them to pause after eleven or twelve sharings just so we could all have a turn. Their delight at having the awareness of all the goodness present in their lives, amidst all the challenges of the year, was heartwarming and humbling for me to hear. It goes without saying that it was part of my gratitude that evening to be honored as a witness to their growth in that way.

The benefits of this simple exercise manifests each day in a number of ways, including reduced bickering with one another over toys; increased sharing of games, books, and computer time; more tenderness towards their mother as she navigates the challenges of managing homeschool activities, family recreation, house management, and her own business; more consideration for the work-at-home logistics their father must adhere to, and a greater level of compassion for their ninety-five-year-old great-nana who they get to see a few times a week.

The calm that gratitude induces at bedtime has made what could be a difficult transition from the digital stimulus of a day much easier and more peaceful for all. I believe it also serves to reinforce feelings of confidence in the world being an abundant place, filled with goodness that is available to us if we simply take time to notice. This awareness does not negate the presence of challenges in life but opens up one's perspective to the opportunities which may be present within them. The ability to creatively analyze situations will serve these youngsters well as they continue their journeys through life.

I share this story to encourage those of you with young ones at home, whether they are six or sixteen, to include them as you try out some of the exercises in the various chapters. The benefits will not only permeate your family, but ripple far beyond the walls of your home.

Teaching gratitude increases awareness, expands compassion, and deepens aspects of resilience that are all much needed qualities in these interesting times.

The New York Times began a weekly series, "Family, Interrupted," in early October 2020 to highlight the impact Covid-19 has had on families, as well as their often challenging and always inspiring coping journeys.

The series demonstrates the need for, and value of, sharing one's story during times of disruption—in the case of 2020, this includes not only the pandemic itself, but the shutdowns resulting from it as well as the wildfires and nationwide civil unrest and protest that have touched every citizen in some way.

Shared stories connect us, strengthen us, build resilience, and expand our individual pool of resources. They provide access to ideas and solutions we may not have previously noticed or even been aware of. They create an atmosphere of solidarity and reflect to us our own strengths that we sometimes ignore or undervalue.

Sharing stories also builds appreciation for the abundances and gifts we do have in our lives and that we have access to through those around us.

BUILD THAT SHARING MUSCLE EXERCISE

Go through your contact lists—the ones you have accumulated on your smartphone, the friends or followers on social media, or, if you're still a bit old school, the stack of business cards you have in a drawer somewhere.

Make an appointment with yourself for one morning or evening per week to reach out to at least 3 to 5 of these contacts.

Be curious as you reach out. Inquire how they are doing. Inquire about their work or their family. Ask about the latest post you've seen from them on Facebook, Instagram, et cetera.

If you call them and get their voicemail, leave a message that you were thinking of them and just wanted to say hi.

If speaking to folks you haven't been in contact with for a while feels a bit awkward, simply set a timer for fifteen minutes, then close the call with, "Take care and be well."

Notice the feelings that arise as you work through your list, as well as the feelings expressed by those you have conversations with. Be open to whatever may emerge as a result.

OTHER IDEAS TO CONSIDER

In these times of unpredictable and sometimes arbitrarily imposed social distancing mandates, it is more important than ever to establish and maintain connection in the most creative ways possible.

For example, there are young people who have initiated writing campaigns for residents of nursing homes that were closed to visitors due to concerns of contamination. This same type of campaign could be energetically useful for our frontline healthcare workers, schoolteachers, emergency responders, and others who find themselves in high-stress scenarios and isolated from the usual communal support structures they may have relied on in the past.

"In a world where you can be anything, be kind."

~ Unknown

The organization Random Acts of Kindness has a series of guidelines for incorporating kindness into school curriculum. They have crafted downloadable lesson plans for pre-school through 12th grade and are gathering data on the impacts seen in school systems that are using their materials. Learning to be kind to others is a brilliant way to build awareness of the value of being kind to oneself as well. This and more is available at randomactsofkindness.org.

GRAPPLING WITH GRIEF / DANCING WITH DEPRESSION

As mentioned throughout this book, change can feel disruptive, disturbing, and heavy, even when it is moving us to brighter, better places. And when that change is unexpected or unwanted or massive in scale, it can also be accompanied by feelings of grief and loss.

Here are some resources we have found to be valuable for clients as they have wrestled with finding groundedness in the midst of upheaval. Some are spiritual in nature, for it is from the depths of our soulspace that we are responding when we find ourselves sad or depressed or even hopeless. Others are more structural in content and supply concrete action steps that will provide relief and ease during times of struggle.

Reach out to others to find out what has been helpful and to reinforce to them, and yourself, that we are all in this together. Solo travel is never a requirement and doesn't work for all of us. Remember "pain shared is halved and joy shared is doubled." If you are finding yourself on the darker side of change, reach out and find connection. Keep reaching until you find something that brings relief.

BOOKS TO CONSIDER:

- *When Things Fall Apart: Heart Advice for Difficult Times* – Pema Chodron, 1997
- *A Path With Heart: A Guide Through the Perils and Promises of Spiritual Life* – Jack Kornfield, 1993
- *I Thought It Was Just Me (But It Isn't)* – Brené Brown, 2007

OTHER RESOURCES:

- **Crisis Text Line** | Text HOME To 741741 free, 24/7 confidential crisis intervention for a range of challenges including anxiety, depression, suicide, and school issues
- **National Suicide Prevention Lifeline** 1-800-273-8255 ~ www.suicidepreventionlifeline.org
- **TrevorText** is a confidential and secure resource that provides live help for LGBTQ youth with a trained specialist, over text messages. Text START to 678-678.
- If you are a young person in crisis, feeling suicidal, or in need of a safe and judgment-free place to talk, call the **TrevorLifeline** now at 1-866-488-7386.

"If the doors of perception were cleansed, everything would appear to man as it is— Infinite."

~ William Blake

Chapter Nine

Connecting With The Infinite

In order to get a more visceral sense of what this discussion of the Infinite might be about, it is helpful to literally "step outside." The contracted spaces we tend to sequester ourselves in, along with the narrowly-focused devices we use to work, play, communicate, and entertain ourselves, can begin to disconnect us from the larger realm of reality that is available to us.

On a beautiful fall Colorado evening, as I was walking home from dinner with some out-of-town guests, I took a moment to point out some celestial events going on in the night sky. My guests, who were visiting from Manhattan, were mesmerized by the clarity of the mostly dark sky environment in our little town here in the mountains. It was just a day after the new moon so the absence of star-dimming moonlight made for easy enjoyment of the Milky Way and other constellations. I pointed out the distinctively bright lights of Jupiter and Saturn in the southern sky and then turned their attention to the east, where Mars was glowing in all its heavenly red brilliance. These brilliant young MIT graduates, now successful entrepreneurs in the commercial software development realm, were in awe of the domain they had never thought to explore before. The simplicity of merely "looking up" struck them as almost too good to be true. They became animated at the prospect of being able to connect so easily with such inspiring beauty and abundance. The conversation quickly went to discussions around trying new things, exploring new information, and curiosity about learning more of what nature has to offer. The magical quality of joy we all shared in those moments is one which is hard to describe but easy to remember the feeling of.

Our access to infinite possibilities is always easier and broader than we imagine. Sometimes it requires abandoning what we have become familiar and comfortable with and setting out into new terrain to explore what else is available.

Beginning to expand our concepts of where life, beauty, and inspiration exist can be as simple as finding a tree to sit under and contemplating how many leaves are on a single branch. Closing one's eyes to tune into the myriad of sounds that exist on a spring day, or any day, is another great way to spark curiosity for what's "out there." Taking time to notice an interesting stone and then allowing our hands to bring us information about the journey it may have gone on before landing in our presence breaks us out of our linear norms for interacting with the world around us. There are several books in the resource section that will further stimulate your creativity in connecting more broadly with the world in which we have landed.

THE VALUE OF COACHING AS A SUPPORT TOOL

By Mark Dockendorff

Trying to follow your own compass and figure out the map to reach your destination can be complicated, confusing, and full of fear. That's why a coach/guide is so valuable for each and every one of us. Some of the stories we included highlight this benefit. A great coach will have an infinite mindset and know that your goal(s) can be useful as tools for inspiration, motivation, and focus. Having the mindset that there is no end to this journey is foundational to being highly curious about what is possible, and gaining clarity about which way to pivot in any given moment, especially in times of chaos. Self-discovery is all about having an honest connection with our innermost selves.

We hope you will take the time to explore some of the resources and books recommended in the Resource section. Over the years of multiple trainings and certifications we have accessed dozens of excellent volumes with valuable information for developing competency in navigating this journey. Most are available in multiple formats—hard copy, electronic, and audio. Have fun perusing the first few chapters online, if possible, to find what might resonate for you and be of value, wherever you currently find yourself.

> *"The good life is a process, not a state of being. It is a direction not a destination."*
>
> ~ Carl Rogers

As a closing gift we have included an image for you to copy or color in place with the vibrancy you wish to see for yourself as you expand your level of engagement with each circle. The concepts we have covered in this book all add depth and dimension to the emotions listed around this Bubble. Spend some time considering how you are bringing vitality to each, then color in the corresponding circle in a way that inspires you. Have fun with it and make the image of your Inspired Journey a bright one!

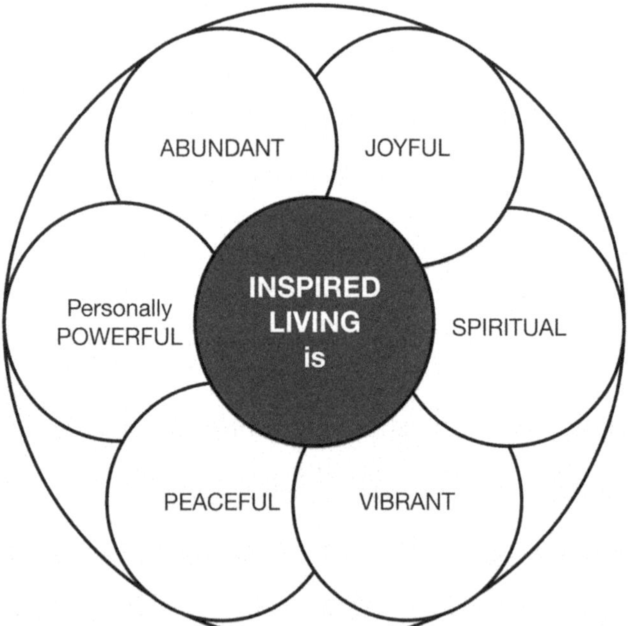

Resources

Chapter One: The Spark

Coaching resources:

Energy Leadership – Bruce D. Schneider, 2008

How To Be, Do, or Have Anything: A Practical Guide To Creative Empowerment – Laurence G. Boldt, 2001

www.ipeccoaching.com

www.oneideaaway.com

www.theinstituteforinspiredliving.org

Chapter Two: Curiosity

Reclaiming The Wild Soul: How Earth's Landscapes Restore Us To Wholeness – Mary Reynolds Thompson, 2014

The Sound of Paper – Julia Cameron, 2004

John Muir: My Life With Nature – Joseph Cornell, 2000

Astrophysics for People in a Hurry – Neil deGrasse Tyson, 2017

Chapter Three: Clarity

Positivity – Barbara L. Frederickson, 2009

Living in Gratitude – Angeles Arrien, 2011, 2013

The Power of Now: A Guide to Spiritual Enlightenment – Eckhart Tolle, 1999

VIA Institute (VIA = Values In Action), Cincinnati, OH

www.viacharacter.org

Chapter Four: Courage

Solo: On Her Own Adventure – ed. Susan Fox Rogers, 2005

Touch The Top of The World – Eric Weihenmayer, 2001

Chapter Five: Congruence

The Little Book of Awakening – Mark Nepo 2000
Change Your Thoughts - Change Your Life: Living the Wisdom of the Tao – Wayne W. Dyer, 2007

Elevating My Business (Zan Marshall Ray and Tom Collins)
www.elevatingmybusiness.com

Video resources for breathing exercises:
www.HoldenQiGong.com
www.JalaBlu.com

Chapter Six: Self-Care

The Miracle of Mindfulness – Thich Nhat Hanh, 1975
Stand Like Mountain, Flow Like Water – Brian Luke Seward, 1997
Mindfulness Meditation in Everyday Life – Jon Kabat-Zinn, 2014 (audiobook)
www.positivepsychology.com/mindfulness-exercises-techniques-activities

Chapter Eight: Reflections on 2020

Creating True Peace – Thich Nhat Hanh, 2003
The Gift of Change – Marianne Williamson, 2004
The Gifts of Imperfection – Brené Brown, 2010

Chapter Nine: Connecting With The Infinite

My First Summer in The Sierra – John Muir, 1911
The Gift – Hafiz
A New Earth – Eckhart Tolle, 2005

About Dr. Moira M. Forsythe

Dr.Moira Forsythe, ND, CPC, ELI-MP, CDLS is an iPEC-certified professional leadership coach and naturopathic practitioner whose passion for empowering others to their best lives has been a central theme for her for over thirty-five years. Moira is nationally certified in several disciplines of holistic practice, at one time having the largest complementary care wellness practice in central Colorado. She has lectured nationally and internationally to large groups on the topic of bioenergetics and lifestyle balance, which ultimately inspired her to develop the coaching practice she has today.

In addition to the CPC, Moira holds professional certifications in Core Dynamics Leadership Coaching, Group Coaching, Energy Leadership Coaching, and Spiritual Network Marketing coaching. She has led transition and empowerment Mastermind groups for entrepreneurs, women, and athletes for over twenty years. Her success with emerging entrepreneurs seeking to change the social culture of the world is making a difference around the globe.

Coming up in the sports era of Title IX for women, Moira has constantly looked for the next biggest challenge in her own athletic pursuits. This has taken her from leading outdoor groups up Mount Whitney in the California Sierra

Mountains to winter expeditions in the White Mountains and high-altitude marathons, mountain biking events, and ultra runs. As she has conquered the milestones within herself she has also sought to bring meaning to her athletic endeavors by riding for the MS 150 Bike event in Colorado, riding her mountain bike across Montana to raise over $7,000 for AIDS research, and organizing local charity runs in California and Colorado over the years.

Most recently she participated in a virtual Summit Challenge, climbing over 15,000 vertical feet in 7 days to support the efforts of the 2020 Coaches That Care initiative.

In addition to her regular trail running at 9,000 feet and her executive coaching practice, Moira was a member of the Crestone Mountain Wisdom Taiko troupe for over eight years, playing year-round throughout Colorado in the name of non-violent communication and world peace. She uses classical labyrinths as a walking meditation tool and is an experienced facilitator of labyrinth workshops. She has installed dozens of labyrinths throughout the US for over twenty-eight years.

She is a contributing author in the teaching guide, *Keys To Conscious Business Growth*, 2016 and was one of 50 elite iPEC coaches selected to facilitate at the international World Happiness Summit held in Miami in 2017.

Moira can be reached at:

level7coaching@gmail.com
coachesthatcare.org

About Mark J. Dockendorff

Mark Dockendorff, CPC, ELI-MP provides innovative ideas to people to support them in understanding and living out their core values. Mark is an Internationally Certified Professional Coach, an Energy Leadership Index - Master Practitioner and a Certified Mediator and Conflict Resolution Specialist, creating coaching partnerships based on trust, loyalty, and accountability. He is a highly intuitive listener who is curious, heart-centered, and non-judgmental.

Mark grew up in Canada surrounded by an abundance of glorious nature, having access to the shores of the great inland sea of Lake Superior. Here he found deep spiritual connection with nature in all its seasons, reconnecting with his own inner knowing as a trusted source of energy and guidance.

Mark's background includes time with Up with People, an inclusive global diversity leadership program that has taken him to thirteen countries, where he submersed into each community by staying with over ninety different host families. His journey has included leadership and accountability coursework at Queen's University in Kingston, Ontario. Mark holds additional "At Work" certifications from UC Berkley in Mindfulness and Resilience, Emotional Intelligence, and the Science of Happiness. Mark has worked in top leadership roles in the social enterprise nonprofit sector. His life-transforming experience as a nut shop owner is included in this book.

Mark currently works with clients one-on-one and in workshops throughout Canada and the United States.

Mark can be reached at:

MarkDockendorff.com
inspired@MarkDockendorff.com

What's Next, Beyond this Book?

The fire has opened the seed of great possibility. 2020 has been the year that has allowed the seed to transform into a greatness of collaboration. Moira and I have been traveling along, collecting all kinds of wonderful resources and find ourselves where our paths have converged. We found ourselves connecting on so many levels of possibility and have had fun creatively exploring how to shape our energy towards a beautiful direction. Knowing that our cause is so much bigger than we are, we are excited to join with others in expanding its reach and effectiveness.

We have joined forces to create a new entity: The Institute for Inspired Living.

The Institute for Inspired Living is shaping to be a space where the magic of true collaboration comes alive and has the capacity to be an example that others will find useful to be inspired by as they emerge with their own brilliance.

We believe that the self-discovery tools we deliver enable people to achieve self-awareness, more competent communication skills, and exciting levels of creativity. This process of identifying core values, creating visions to live into, and developing strategic plans facilitates the process of advancing systemic change both personally and societally. By empowering individuals, we can help transform the collective culture, impacting the current and future state of the world.

We are currently working on a book club guide to be available for readers of *Infinite Journey* by January 2021. It will support the collaborative exploration and development of some of the concepts herein on a broader level. Send us an email to receive the guide.

Inspiredlivinginstitute2020@gmail.com
Facebook.com/theinstituteforinspiredliving
@theinstituteforinspiredliving

The Institute for Inspired Living

Empowering Expanded Mindsets

Optimizing the Human Experience

www.i4il.org • info@i4il.org

Made in USA - Kendallville, IN
1216583_9781735657912
12.22.2020 0759